Trying to Explain

DONALD DAVIE

Trying
to
Explain

Poets on Poetry

Donald Hall, General Editor

Trying to Explain

DONALD DAVIE

Ann Arbor   The University of Michigan Press

Published in the United States of America by
The University of Michigan Press and simultaneously
in Rexdale, Canada, by John Wiley & Sons Canada, Limited
Manufactured in the United States of America

Library of Congress Cataloging in Publication Data

Davie, Donald.
   Trying to explain.

   (Poets on poetry)
   1. American poetry—20th century—History and
criticism—Collected works.   2. English poetry—
20th century—History and criticism—Collected
works.   I. Title.   II. Series.
PS323.5.D3   821'.9'109   79-16422
ISBN 0-472-06310-3

Preface

Here are some periodical pieces, mostly rather recent, which concern themselves with poetry both American and British, from the point of view of a British poet who has, however, resided for the past ten years in the United States. Like most of my contemporaries among poets, whether British or American, I've spent a lot of time on the campuses not as a temporary visitor, for instance as "Writer in Residence," but as a full-time scholar and teacher—in Ireland and England as well as the United States. So, if it seems that I talk about poetry more as a professor than as a poet, I can only say that in my experience the two vocations come together; a way of talking that may seem "professorial" or "academic" seems to me the right and proper way, or at any rate *one* of the right and proper ways, for a writer to talk about writing when he hopes to be heard by those, academic or nonacademic, who are writers themselves, and take writing as seriously as he does.

Donald Davie

Contents

Theme and Action

Of Allen Tate's poem "The Buried Lake" (1953), it has been rightly said that it "appeared just as a new poetry began to rise in America":

> This new poetry's obsessions with oratory, romantic gesture, and exhibitionism have . . . altered the way poetry works in the modern world. Even some of Tate's friends shifted eventually toward the new mode, among them Robert Penn Warren, Robert Lowell, and John Berryman.

This "new mode" is as firmly established still as it was when Radcliffe Squires wrote of it thus in 1971. There are no signs that it has run its course, or is likely to do so at all soon. And accordingly public taste is no better prepared for Tate's *Collected Poems 1919-1976* than it was for his *Poems* (1960). Not many poets in any time have had to survive for so many years a change in taste (or in fashion) which so comprehensively brought into disrepute all, or nearly all, that the poet in question had set most store by in his art. It is an unenviable fate; and Allen Tate deserves our sympathy. I shall argue that he deserves a great deal more than that; but sympathy at least is what none of us should deny him.

As for the drastic change in expectations which put

This essay first appeared in *Parnassus* 6, no. 2 (1978).

Tate in mid-career out of key with his age and his public, the most telling sign of it, to my mind, is that in all the four hundred pages of Tate's forty-five-year-long literary correspondence with Donald Davidson the name of William Carlos Williams rates not a single entry, whereas belated admiration for Williams's performance in poetry has been perhaps the defining characteristic of the years from 1953 to the present day—a development inaugurated if by any one person then by Randall Jarrell, a Vanderbilt man like Tate, and at one time quite close to him. By contrast, among Tate's contemporaries and associates through earlier decades, only Yvor Winters I think made any claims for Williams's poetry, and those claims were much more severely qualified than what it has become usual to claim for him through the last quarter-century. This sudden but sustained veneration for the author of *Paterson* could not help but damage Tate's relations with his readers. For Williams struggled—in the end very successfully—to present American readers with an either/or choice between his sort of poetry and T. S. Eliot's; whereas by 1953 Tate had for many years conspicuously aligned himself with Eliot—with Eliot's world view, however, more than with Eliot's verse style.

If it be objected that Radcliffe Squires's formulations—"oratory, romantic gesture, and exhibitionism"—point somewhere away from Williams, I would for my part contend rather vigorously that Williams's performance answers to all these prescriptions: it *is* oratorical, it *does* make romantic gestures, and it *is* exhibitionist. I could even be quite bitter about it. For I can still recapture the sense of inexcusable affront that I had twenty-five years ago in England when, having learned to esteem American poetry in the work of Tate and John Crowe Ransom, and having worked out from that bridgehead to make more or less rewarding contact with Hart Crane, with Winters, and the early Penn Warren, I found myself made a monkey of, asked to esteem what seemed by contrast the unlicked and *faux-naïf* writing of Williams's *Collected Earlier Poems*. I remain convinced today that a sort of sentimental populism in Williams himself, in an influential admirer like Jarrell, and among American readers generally, overrates Williams's sort of poetry, and is grievously unfair to the incompatible sort of poetry that Allen Tate has written.

I cannot help being personal. For like any other literary man of my generation in the English-speaking world I find myself, as I turn the pages of Tate's *Collected Poems*, repeatedly brought up short by poems and parts of poems that recall my past to me—so constantly, though by no means always consciously, has Tate been a presence in my thinking from the time when I first began considering what serious writing might be. That presence was always minatory and challenging, never reassuring. The demands which it made of writing and of writers (also of readers) were always far too exacting for comfort. As early as 1929 the author of *Mr. Pope and Other Poems*, published the previous year, wrote to Donald Davidson from Paris:

> Tradition is the intensest expression, or communication, the past has reached. This is always difficult. What most people mean by tradition is the debased and diluted version of the great masters which the second rate poets have passed on. Like Tennyson. It is worthy of remark that the only Victorian poet who is in the great tradition (Arnold) is put aside for Browning and Tennyson. These latter give the reader all the illusion of reading poetry, without forcing him to extend himself to the great effort of reading poetry itself. It is almost as difficult to read poetry as it is to write it. I find it so, and so should the reader, I believe.

In 1929 there was perhaps some excuse for this. And in fact there is an account of an older Tate teaching "Tears,

Idle Tears" in Minnesota, which suggests that he was not always so disrespectful to Tennyson. But it was surely wrong in 1929, as it was less excusably wrong in 1940 when I heard something similar from my teachers in England, and as it is quite inexcusably wrong in 1978, to relegate Tennyson to the second rate and elevate Arnold above him. In short, the Whitmanesque strain in American poetry was not the only legacy from the past which Tate exhorted us to disown, and sometimes when we of my generation bowed to his authority we cheated ourselves out of certain bequests that we have only lately and at some cost recovered for ourselves. And so the powerful presence that speaks to us from these poems was not always in the past beneficent. The "tradition" that Tate proudly claimed to prolong and to speak for was less capacious than it should have been.

It was the same when one turned from Tate's criticism to his poems. Those too one regarded with respect and even awe, but hardly with love. Particularly if one read them, as I did, along with Ransom's, one could not fail to remark in them the lack of that seductive suavity which won us over to Ransom. The "great effort" required of us as readers was apparent; what was not clear was the payoff, quite simply the pleasure, that our efforts were supposed to earn. Ransom, Hart Crane, even in his austere way Winters, were *winning* writers in a way that Tate has seldom deigned to be. That winningness which these others had, which he disdained, might take the form of haunting and plangent cadence; but equally it could be no more than the explicit making of common cause with his readers, by alerting them to a topic or an occasion which they could share with him, either actually or in imagination. Thus, when a poem called "Picnic at Cassis" was dauntingly retitled "The Mediterranean," the reader was denied the chance of making common cause with the poet in the familiar occasion signified by "picnic"; and he was left to work out for himself that something as familiar as a picnic was being talked of—no easy matter, after a cunningly adapted epigraph from Virgil, and in view of the grand sonority of the diction:

> Let us lie down once more by the breathing side
> Of Ocean, where our live forefathers sleep
> As if the Known Sea still were a month wide—
> Atlantis howls but is no longer steep!
>
> What country shall we conquer, what fair land
> Unman our conquest and locate our blood?
> We've cracked the hemispheres with careless hand!
> Now, from the Gates of Hercules we flood
>
> Westward, westward till the barbarous brine
> Whelms us to the tired land where tasseling corn,
> Fat beans, grapes sweeter than muscadine
> Rot on the vine: in that land were we born.

The point is not in the least that this grand diction is excessive for recounting a boating picnic by expatriate Americans in the south of France; on the contrary, the truly imaginative act was precisely in moving from an occasion so trivial to a peroration so grand and yet so well earned, and the winningness of that progression, that "rise," was forfeited as soon as the intrinsically trivial occasion was suppressed, or buried so deep that we have to delve to find it. This is a great pity. For these verses are very moving, and incidentally exemplify—consider the inventive vigor inside the pentameter—how Tate could adopt the world view of the American Virgilian expatriate Eliot, while being not in the least indebted to Eliot in movement through the verse line, or from verse to verse. Great and memorable as it is, this poem of 1933 still suffers from having (perversely as it must seem) curtailed the imaginative movement from the particular to the general, by ill-advised second thoughts concealing the particularity of the occasion it started from.

An even more striking and regrettable instance of this perversity is the ambitious poem in four parts, "Seasons of the Soul" (1944). The four parts, headed "Summer," "Autumn," "Winter," "Spring," can be, and have been, glossed in other terms: for instance, "Air," "Earth," "Water," and "Fire"; also the soul of man (1) as political figure, (2) as abandoned sufferer, (3) as sexual being, (4) as desperately appealing before death for spiritual insight. But what is there in the poem, as immediately experienced by the reader, which could tempt him to consult the erudite commentaries—by Vivienne Koch, for instance, and Katherine Garrison Chapin—which tease out these further "levels"? (And what a whiff of the recent past, by the way, comes up from that very word, "levels"!) Well, there is this, as early as the third stanza:

> It was a gentle sun
> When, at the June solstice
> Green France was overrun
> With caterpillar feet.
> No head knows where its rest is
> Or may lie down with reason
> When war's usurping claws
> Shall take the heart escheat—
> Green field in burning season
> To stain the weevil's jaws.

But that vivid evocation of the 1940 blitzkrieg on France is the only concession that Tate makes to his reader, to advise him that the immediate occasion of the poem is one that he shares with the poet—the experience of World War II. And without Donald Davidson's privileged insight ("the four parts . . . as reflecting *throughout* the disastrous implications of World War II"), how would any of us identify—among the distracting echoes of Virgil and Dante, Wyatt and Lucretius and Traherne—*submarines* as the subject of the second stanza of "Winter":

> A shark swift as your dove
> Shall pace our company
> All night to nudge and tear
> The livid wound of love?

Once again, as in "The Mediterranean," the particular occasion of the poem, instead of being made to release symbolic or emblematic resonances, is suppressed *in favor of* those resonances—with the result that every reader, except the most attentive and instructed, will hear those resonances bombinating in a void. As with "The Mediterranean," so here with "Seasons of the Soul" we have a poem of very great accomplishment (the siren song here is Yeats, the Yeats of "The Tower," as there it was Eliot) erecting quite gratuitous and perverse obstructions between itself and the well-disposed reader.

With this endemic fault (for so I take it) there goes another, which is graver since it concerns not the poet's relation with his reader but his relation with his language. Cleanth Brooks detected it many years ago, though without reprobation. "Almost every adjective in his poetry," said Brooks, "challenges the reader's imagination to follow it off at a tangent." Typical instances in "The Mediterranean" are "a gull white-winged along the *feckless* wave," and "When lust of power undid its *stuffless* rage" (NED knows no such word as "stuffless"); from "Seasons of the Soul," "time's *engaging* jaws," and (an ill-judged acquisition from Thomas Wyatt)

> I saw my downcast mother
> Clad in her street-clothes,
> Her blue eyes *long* and *small*. . . .

And then there are the three terza rima poems of the 1950s (three parts of a projected autobiographical poem, planned first to have nine parts, later six). Here we find, in the first of them, "The Maimed Man":

> . . . By eye I mean the busy, *lurked*, discrete
> Mandible world sharp as a broken tooth.)
>
> And then rose in the man a small half-hell
> Where love disordered, shade of *pompous* youth,
> Clutched shades forbearing in a family well; . . .

where the dictionary gives no warrant for "lurk" as a transitive verb, and where "pompous" is there for a pun with the Greek *'pompos* as applied to Hermes. And the second poem, "The Swimmers," begins:

> Kentucky water, clear springs: a boy fleeing
> To water under the dry Kentucky sun,
> His four little friends in tandem with him, seeing
>
> Long shadows of grapevine wriggle and run
> Over the green swirl; mullein under the ear
> Soft as Nausicaa's palm; *sullen* fun
>
> *Savage* as childhood's *thin harmonious* tear: . . .

—where every one of the last four adjectives seems indeed, in Brooks's sense, "tangential," and thereby as far as possible from what Pound applauded in Johnson's "Vanity of Human Wishes": "the lexicographer's weighing of the epithet." In fact, this persistent mannerism in Tate's verse ought to give pause not only to those who too readily describe it as "classical," but also to those who describe it as "modern"—insofar as "the modern" in Anglo-American verse may be thought to derive as much from Pound's precedent as from Eliot's.

What I am suggesting is that the besetting fault of Tate's writing, early and late, has been an impatient neglect of the literal meaning of his poems in favor of their symbolical or (his own word) *anagogical* meanings. To give just one more instance, in the very beautiful "Shadow and Shade" of 1933—a poem admired by Winters though by few others, and another that stands at least as far from Eliot as from Williams—the only flaw, though a serious one, is the impossibility of knowing where the two actors in the poem are standing (indoors, that is, or out-of-doors).

And I believe this may be the point to engage with Tate's identity as a Southerner—though a captious and restive one. For it seems to be characteristic of the literature of the Southern Renascence—of that literature, and of the criticism which attended and explained it up to Walter Sullivan's remarkable *Death by Melancholy* (1972)—that it insists on "theme," as distinct or distinguishable from "action." This distinction, it has been pointed out, has no justification in any Aristotelean scheme, though other components of that scheme (for instance "plot" and "character") are taken over by Southern critics. But in any case the distinction offends against common sense. For all the critical commentaries agree that the stories and poems of the Southern Renascence have one theme, and one only: the myth—by which one does not mean the fiction, still less the illusion—of an antebellum Southern civilization destroyed by the Civil War, or by that war's aftermath. To be sure, there were distinct shadings in the different retellings of the myth: differences, for instance, about how far the seeds of its destruction were in the antebellum South from the first; or again, more urgently, differences about what should be the attitude and the aspirations of the self-conscious Southerner in the here and now of the 1930s and 1940s. But these were only shadings; the myth was massively one and the same, so we were told, in Andrew Lytle's *The Long Night* and in Tate's "Aeneas at Washington." But if that were so, and if the theme were what one read for, why bother reading Mr. Lytle's novel when one had read Mr. Tate's poem, or vice versa? Since it's a fact of experience that a reading of the one work doesn't spoil one for the other, it follows that what one reads for and responds to isn't in the first place the theme, but on the contrary, in Aristotle's sense, the *action*.

It is obviously easier to detect the action in a narrative or a drama than in a poem like "Aeneas at Washington" which is not in any usual sense either narrative or dramatic. Yet every poem of any sort *has* an action—an action consisting of the sequence of its words and images exploding on the reader's consciousness, now fast, now slow, now pushing forward, now circling back. The action, of course, need not be continuous, but will develop through stages, incorporating a jump or break from one stage to the next. In a scrupulous poet like Tate, we may expect to find such "jumps" indicated by typography. So it is in "Aeneas at Washington" where, after the first sixteen lines of magnificent (and yes, winning) translation and adaptation from the *Aeneid*, there is a break signaled by a space and the beginning of a parenthesis:

> (To the reduction of uncitied littorals
> We brought chiefly the vigor of prophecy,
> Our hunger breeding calculation
> And fixed triumphs.)

For Lillian Feder these four lines are "a brilliant transition"; but she can think so because she is reading the poem for its theme, and thus can gloss it from Tate's essays. But if it should be read, like any other poem, for its *action*, does not the abrupt desertion of the pentameter in the first and third of these lines make one hear in the diction the Eliot of "Gerontion"? And in that case, does this not strike us as a parenthesis in a damaging sense, not a resumption or a switching of the action, but a standing aside from it, not a break in the action but a damaging breach of it, a wandering of attention, both ours and the poet's?

The action then resumes, magnificently. The destroyed South is named in "Blue Grass," rammed hard against "Troy" in controlled synaesthesia bringing conflagration and fruition together. The action now is indeed "explosive" and rapid:

> I saw the thirsty dove
> In the glowing fields of Troy, hemp ripening
> And tawny corn, the thickening Blue Grass
> All lying rich forever in the green sun.

There is to my ear a lapse three lines later into telltale sub-Eliotic diction signaled by the mannered epithet, "singular":

> The singular passion
> Abides its object and consumes desire
> In the circling shadow of its appetite . . .

—lines which Cleanth Brooks, reading for "theme" as Lillian Feder did with the parenthesis, can seem to vindicate by a gloss from Tate's essay, "Religion and the Old South." But after that the action proceeds with authority and magnificence to its tragic conclusion when the speaker on the banks of the Potomac asserts bleakly:

> Struck in the wet mire
> Four thousand leagues from the ninth buried city
> I thought of Troy, what we had built her for.

("Struck," I'm afraid, is a misprint for "stuck.")

Thus, even in this, which I take to be one of the great

poems of our time and one of the greatest American poems of all time, there are flaws more or less damaging. And this seems to be the rule: if I were asked to name any one poem by Mr. Tate that is flawlessly consummated, I doubt if I could find one. But what follows from that? Only that in the act of composition he is mastered by forces which he can only with difficulty, and not consistently, master. It is a sort of definition of what an older criticism would recognize as a poet of genius, rather than talent. Tate as critic and pedagogue has had a noble contempt for the too easy understanding of the artist as one who knows not what it is he does; yet his own work shows that he too, despite his analytic intelligence and his principled civic responsibility, was, when he wrote his greatest poems, carried out of himself, overmastered. Properly to take leave of him, we need not prose but verse. Conceivably, thus:

> Rue for remembrance: not
> A tribute he would slight.
> And yet of us he asks
> That what we say be right.

> The Man of Letters as
> Hero was not the mark
> He aimed at, but it was
> The chaplet of Petrarch.

> Praise then no scrupulous voice
> That chose, and chose right. Those
> The Muse takes have no choice;
> He was of those she chose.

Steep Trajectories

I have been enthusiastic about Ed Dorn's writing ever since I was introduced by the Englishman J. H. Prynne to Dorn's first collection of poems, *The Newly Fallen* (1961). I have followed him since through *Hands Up!* (1964) and *The North Atlantic Turbine* (1967—Dorn's "European" book); also through the prose books *The Rites of Passage* (1965), *The Shoshoneans* (1966), and *Some Business Recently Transacted in the White World* (1971). A book which stands rather apart from all these, but very valuable, is *Recollections of Gran Apacheria* (1974). As for Dorn's most ambitious undertaking to date, which occupied him from 1967 to 1974, the comic and visionary narrative poem *Gunslinger* (called *Slinger* when it came out from Berkeley in 1975), I did my best to keep abreast of it as its four books appeared one by one over those years, but it's a difficult work and I've never yet given myself the opportunity to take it in as a whole.

My enthusiasm for this body of writing is one that I've been able to share with very few of my friends, whether British or American. And I understand why. Dorn's latest

This review first appeared in 1978 in the Vanderbilt Campus magazine, *Maxie's Journal,* edited by Craig Chambers.

collection, *Hello, La Jolla*, for instance, will move most of my friends to exasperation, and some to apoplexy. What are they to make (I hear them snarl) of misspellings like "exhuberant," "who's" for "whose," "eminent" (for, apparently, "immanent"), "queezy," "idealogical," "footbol," "catagorize," "practise" (for "practice"), "feignt" (for "feint"), "permenantum" (for, apparently, "permanentum"), "oecological," "thorobred," "nickle-plated," "emmigrate," "excitment"? Are these misspellings deliberate? (Some are; others I think aren't.) Are they misprints? (Again, some are, some aren't.) Wasn't there a poet (Eliot) who said that poetry must be "at least as well written as good prose"? And haven't poets from as far back as Dante forward through Ben Jonson taken as one of their responsibilities the provision of a model of propriety and serviceable correctness to all other users of language? Where then but in California (I hear my friends splutter) would one find, elegantly printed on good paper, the misspellings listed above, or a complete poem like Dorn's "A Sense of Place"?

> I'd live on the Moon
> if the commute were
> a little less.

What is this but the new barbarism, Walt Whitman's "barbaric yawp" updated and even more raucous, an impudent fraud on a reading public either too uneducated to notice it is being conned, or else too cowed and disoriented to protest?

I sympathize with these friends of mine. Indeed, so far as they are British, I agree with them. Dorn's practice is indeed, and cannot help being, an affront to the British tradition in writing—and this despite the fact that Dorn has lived in England, has been happy there, has collaborated with an Englishman on translating from the Spanish, and has indeed a British-educated wife. It's just because Dorn knows England well, and is at ease among the English, that he defines his own tradition, and indeed his own language, as firmly distinct from theirs—as *American*. It's as an American addressing a fellow American that he says to his interviewer:

> Our articulation is quite different from other people's; we arrive at understanding and meaning through massive assaults on the language, so no particular word is apt to be final. It's rapidly rerun all the time. And I think that can be healthy usage. On the other hand, there's so much of it that it gets the reputation for being loose. A lot of it in fact is.

And this means that if my American friends, for instance Tennesseans, are affronted by Dorn's way of writing, they are in a more awkward situation than the Englishmen. Is Dorn just wrong about American speech habits? Is he mistaking Californian usage for American usage? Hardly; *Hello, La Jolla* is emphatically a Californian book, but Dorn himself isn't Californian; he is as much at home in Chicago, Idaho, Colorado, New Mexico (all of them places he has lived in). Besides, there are Californians—notably those influenced by the late Yvor Winters—who will be as affronted by this book as any Tennessean could be. And finally, if I may turn the knife in the wound, a poem out of Tennessee like Robert Penn Warren's "Pursuit" ("The hunchback on the corner, with gum and shoe-laces") seems to my English ear, though it rhymes and so on, and despite its incidental splendors, demonstrably "loose" in the way that Dorn tolerantly describes.

How Dorn can tolerate such looseness—metrical, grammatical, lexical—in his own work and the work of others comes clear from other passages in the interview, for instance where he says, "My attitude toward writing is that I handle the language every day like a material, and I keep it in *interesting* repair. I don't really care about *good* repair." This of course leaves it open for someone to retort that in American poetry as in any other, while some writers may go to work as Dorn does, there have to be others who perform the Jonsonian function of keeping the language in *good* repair. (Dorn himself might agree.) And when Dorn makes the same point again, saying "I'm always roadtesting the language for a particular form of speech," another retort is possible: Why "speech"? Isn't American English a written, as well as a spoken, language? And why should the spoken language have an automatic priority for the poet, over the written? Dorn might even concede this point too, but reluctantly I think; for he's convinced of the unexploited possibilities in American speech, and eloquent about it, as when he explains the ironic or sarcastic inflection of much of his *Gunslinger*: "It seems to me that our speech is not nearly as flexible as it ought to be, that its potential hasn't been realized, and I would seek in that poem to elevate it from its eternally Flat Trajectories."

At any rate, "interesting repair" is what Dorn claims to do for the spoken American that is his chosen language in this book. And I think he is as good as his word. Jokes and puns, bizarre collocations overheard and imagined—these are his stock in trade; and they are more than "interesting." They are entertaining and also instructive, so long as we recognize that "correctness" isn't the point (we are listening to American speech as it is, not as conceivably it *should be*), and so long as we remember also how comedy can be a way of discussing seriously very serious matters (like transplant surgery, which is the subject of several poems here.)

It must also be said that Dorn is not, like other poets who seem to be on a similar tack, in any way an aggressive know-nothing who wants to deride and reject the English and European inheritance. *Hello, La Jolla* reveals that he has been reading Edward Gibbon and William Cobbett. And he *does* sometimes use the written rather than the spoken language. It is probably my British and literary conditioning that makes me like him best when he does so, as in these lines from a poem about the current opening up of Alaska:

> The creatures of ice feignt and advance
> with a consciousness a great deal more
> pervasive then the rise and fall of wages.
> The tremendous pitch of their crystal stacks
> the vast smell of their lunar coldness
> the mammoth draft of their freezing humidity
> the highminded groan of their polar turns . . .

The misspelling "feignt" is one that is undoubtedly deliberate, and justifiable: in a way that has nothing to do with speech and everything to do with writing, it packs two meanings into the one word, just as (to take another example) "pitch" in line four is the pitch of a ship but also (and more) the pitch of a roof.

The book will do harm if it gets into the wrong hands? No doubt of it. But who ever thought that poetry is a safe commodity? The stuff is dynamite!

A West Riding Boyhood

In California, one summer afternoon in 1971, soon after my forty-ninth birthday, I slept and had a dream. I dreamed that I was walking with my father, who is dead, and my older son, who is now a father himself but in the dream was a child. I remember thinking, in the dream itself or else at the moment of waking, that a collier would speak of him as "my little lad." And in the dream we were among the collieries, in the South Yorkshire of my boyhood. Rawmarsh was the name that came into my head, and certainly Rawmarsh is a place in that neighborhood, though I'm not sure that I've ever been there. As the dream began, I decided suddenly that I was going "home," and I plunged away from my dad and my little lad, rushing and sliding on my own through a scene that is common enough in those parts—old pit hills or slag heaps, tilted steeply one against another, quite bare and sterile, with a narrow defile between them. The sun was blazing, it was very hot, and I knew it was Sunday morning. The spoil, the slag, was not grey-black but reddish, as it can be sometimes. And on I pelted, on and down, the red slopes getting steeper on each side of me, and the path between them, beaten hard, getting more straitened.

This article first appeared in *Prose* 7, 1973.

I came to a faint fork and careered, without deliberation, to the left. And then I stopped, suddenly assailed with a sort of horror—at the heat, the redness all around, the emptiness, and being alone.

It impressed me all of a sudden that I had come the wrong way, so I turned, rushed back uphill, and took the other arm of the fork. And yet, oddly, as I swung around I seemed to see from the tail of my eye that a gable end showed itself down the narrow pass I was turning from, and not so far down either. But that was as it might be, I thought; for the other fork soon brought me among houses which it seemed that I knew and could name as Darfield—an actual village, and one that I knew well enough, though not the precise scene that my dream presented to me. A collier, in choking collar and stiff suit for Sunday, came walking there with his "little lad." And as I approached them, the boy said something which I could not catch, though it must have been a plea for ice cream. For the father answered, not unkindly, "Ice cream? Theer's thi ice cream," pointing to the flagstones black and cool in the shadows of shuttered houses. The place was a spacious yard—in the Yorkshire sense of the word, not the American—at a street's end, with houses round it on three sides, or maybe only on two. "Come in here," the collier said to me; and the sun came in there, hot again, in a bare shop that he must have unlocked, there on the unshadowed side of the square. He leaned on the counter, a telephone to his ear; but I was saying, "I don't need the bus. Just show me the road to Barnsley. I'm going to walk." He was a big strong fellow, and though he had doffed his jacket, the sweat was streaking his red arms from under the rolled-up sleeves of his red-striped shirt. But I didn't care any more; it couldn't be far to Barnsley. And in any case I was safe with him.

Like any dream, this one can be construed. But I suspect a dream yields instruction only if we duck around the allegories that it seems to promise, and come into the shafts of light that it throws out obliquely. And thus the first thing that I'm made to realize about myself, with this dream in mind, is how constantly, throughout my boyhood but also ever since, my strongest and most common emotion has been fear. Fear, or else perhaps apprehension; for the fear has not been of any one thing or person, not even of any definable happening, but always unlocalized, unfocused, pervasive. I have been a coward before life; always, against the run of the evidence, I have expected the worst. Reading John Masefield's *So Long to Learn*, I notice how his childhood was also hedged about with fears, but with fears that could be named—bulls, hornets, adders, the gypsies—and how each of these fears, sharpened and inculcated by the prohibitions or warnings of grown-ups, had a sort of twisted reason to it, either in the actual conditions of nineteenth-century rural England or in past conditions still preserved in the folk memory. My fears were not of that kind; they were always of the unknown, just as now they are of the unforeseeable. My parents were not only kind, but also enlightened; they were sure that only cruel or unenlightened parents peopled a child's world with bogies. It was not they who fed my fears. No one fed them. They throve on a spectral diet, and might even have shrunk a little if they had had something corporeal to bite on.

The only material fear that I can remember is of "rough boys," who were to be recognized in Barnsley about 1930 because they wore jerseys (and also, the roughest of them, wooden clogs), whereas gentle or gentlemanly or nice boys wore blouses, as I did. But this was not a serious fear, and did not survive a day when my worst tormentor turned out to wear a blouse and to be shod in sandals. Barnsley society, as it was known to a schoolboy, was rigorously simplified and, as I see now, truncated: there were only two classes—proletariat and petty bourgeois. Attorneys, clergymen, doctors (though not dentists) sent their children away to boarding schools; and so, effectively, in St. Mary's School there were only the sons of colliers and the sons of small shopkeepers like my father. (It comes to me now that the sons of artisans, of carpenters for instance, were classified sartorially as jersey-wearers or blouse-wearers; we had our own sumptuary laws, though they were flexible.) Barnsley was a society so overwhelmingly proletarian that it always was, as it still is, an impregnable Labour stronghold in both municipal and national politics. We always voted the other ticket, without hope. And at times I have indulged the notion that, growing up thus in a disfranchised minority, and learning at my mother's knee the inevitable tension between us the few and them the many, I was conditioned to a political attitude that used to be called *Poujadiste*; and I have fancied that I detected in myself the sentiments of a petty bourgeois fascist. My dream is welcome to me because it disproved that. Perhaps it even disproves the Marxist theory of classes. For in the dream my Samaritan was undeniably proletarian, beneficent, and to be trusted, a protector.

It would be odd if it were otherwise. For my mother herself was born in a colliery cottage; and though my maternal grandfather, John Sugden, ended his days (rheumatically and before I was born) as a colliery under-manager, he must have begun—I now realise—at the pit-face. So too my grandfather Davie had come north out of Dorset as a signalman with the railway. And both my grandmothers had been domestic servants. To be sure they had all "bettered themselves"; and though I don't remember that expression being used in my childhood, plainly the idea behind it was still potent in my parents' generation, and even indeed in my own. How ingrained it is in the English, and how tediously mean-minded, this game of class distinctions! I'm ashamed to find it is a game that I still play myself, as these comments show.

The slag-heap scenery of my dream is one that as a child I often walked through, most often with my father, and mostly on a Sunday. We lived on Dodworth Road, and I remember, out of many, two short walks in particular that led through slag heaps: one cut through between Dodworth and Higham, heading towards Hugsett Woods and Silkstone; and the other went through Dodworth and past Gilroyd to Stainbrough. This second one, though it was longer, was better, because near Gilroyd it passed by a tunnel under a railway where one could sometimes see what was then the most powerful locomotive in England hauling coal wagons up the gradient. And Stainbrough, when one got to it, was not a mining village but manorial, sparsely grouped at the gates of the great park round Stainbrough Hall. There were plenty of pockets like that, green and pastoral and manorial, among the industrial wastes. Indeed, if I were to measure the acreage of each kind, discounting, for instance, the fumes from the one that blew across the other, it would be the industrialized acres that would count as the pockets. We, my brother and I, were very early educated to this sort of accountancy, measuring the greater attractiveness of one walk over another according as the proportion of the one kind of landscape to the other was greater or less. And yet I think none of us—my mother and father no more than us children—truly experienced the slag-heap scenery as ugly, a privation, an image of sterility. Thus, although the red landscapes of my dream plead to be construed as infernal, I distrust the allegory here also. Though my dreamed-of panic among them was sharp and frightening, I suspect that panic was what it was—a fear of the empty and the other, of the great god Pan, strange as that must seem. For I remember vividly the initiation rite which I imposed on myself, at puberty I suppose: a Sunday walk *on my own*, through trees, through Hugsett Woods in fact, the unformed and nameless horrors crowding at me, just as they are supposed to do, from among the mossy boles. That, it seemed to me, was the prefiguring of what I experienced in dreaming. Pan, I conclude, dwells for me as much in industrial landscapes as in sylvan ones. And panic in that strict sense is an experience that I know too well; I experience it still, as I did a few months ago in Calaveras Big Trees, California.

About the slag heaps we were, I suppose, in two minds. Certainly my mother was. In her the discrepancy was very striking, and informed her feelings about the West Riding in general. She was fiercely loyal to the Riding, and too ready to see and resent slights upon it in the talk of people we knew who lived in Barnsley but had been raised in other parts of England. And yet it was she, I think, who planted in me the conviction that my native landscape was a sort of aberration; that the norm which it distorted, though it could be perceived in places like Stainbrough, was serenely and securely to be found only elsewhere, outside the West Riding altogether. The reason was, I now believe, that in the tiny, very literary group of us, she was the most literary. For the truth was, of course, that in English literature one found many an image of Stainbrough, but none of Gilroyd or Darfield. This has changed. The poems and stories in Ted Hughes's *Crow* or his *Wodwo* take place in a scenery which is that of my dream; and in fact Ted Hughes was reared in just my neighborhood. But thirty or forty years ago there were only Arnold Bennett and D. H. Lawrence—my mother read both these authors—to suggest, partially and uncertainly, that our industrially ravaged landscape was being assimilated and acknowledged by the English imagination. If English literature imparted wisdom and instruction, as we were sure it did, that wisdom could not be separated from the manorial or pastoral images in which, time and again, it had been conveyed.

My mother was literary because it was through English literature, particularly English poetry, that she had risen from a colliery cottage to be a certificated schoolteacher, without benefit of college training. But that gives the wrong impression. With her, as she might have said herself, English poetry was a passion. She had by heart the greater part, perhaps all, of *The Golden Treasury*, as well as much of Shelley, Browning, Tennyson, others. Tags of verses from Keats and Wordsworth, Shelley and Browning, were always in her mouth; and she was "up with" twentieth-century poets like Flecker and de la Mare, Masefield and Bridges, Drinkwater and W. H. Davies, Newbolt and Noyes. If I am so literary myself that I sometimes despair of breaking through a cocoon of words to a reality outside them, that is above all my mother's doing. And I am grateful; if my universe is verbal, so be it—I am happy in my glittering envelope, and will fight those who would puncture it.

My father, at the times that I remember best, was working long hours to keep his head and ours above water. I am speaking of the Depression. So he had no time for reading, and I thought him less literary than my mother. But if my copy of Burns is a first prize awarded to Alice Sugden of the Sheffield Road Baptist Sunday School, my poetical works of Cowper was in the same year, 1914, a first prize awarded to George C. Davie after a tennis tournament of the Park Tennis Club, Stainbrough. And I see now that their literariness was one thing that must have brought my parents together; I guess indeed that it was romantic literature, doubtless Sir Walter Scott, that impelled my father when he joined the colors in 1915 to enlist in the Highland Light Infantry. In later years when he had more leisure, he once again read a great deal, often substantial works of biography and history. And he too always quoted favorite and for him sacred passages, such as Wolsey's speech from Shakespeare's *Henry VIII*—"Had I but served my God with half the zeal I served my King . . ."

John Masefield wrote of himself as one "who belonged to a literary time, when all read much, and often found the delightful spoil of so much reading a hindrance when they came to tell a tale." My mother and my father were representatives of that "literary time," determined and zealous recruits to the idea of a literary civilization, each of them sprung from a family and a level of English society to which that idea had not penetrated earlier. They survived to know the very different world that had been heralded, before either of them was born, when a French poet had exhorted his fellows to "take literature and wring its neck." Though in fact my mind is laced through with tags and allusions less than theirs were, nevertheless, because I was willingly conditioned by their example, I seem to others and sometimes to myself to be an anachronistic survival from that literary time, living and writing after them in a world in which the idea of a literary civilization is discredited and mocked almost universally, and through times in which the gap between that ideal and any achievable social reality is wider than they could ever have imagined. Masefield is right, of course, and so was Verlaine; the literariness choked or sapped the literary talents of that time—Maurice Hewlett's, Masefield's own, even R. L. Stevenson's. Ezra Pound has come to be for me the great example of how a stubborn talent could force its way through that underbrush; for Pound, Maurice Hewlett's friend, was more literary than any of them. And I will be stubborn too, in maintaining and trying to prove that a passion for past literature, if it sometimes grows up into such strangling entanglements, can also bear bright and sustaining fruit. That is one reason why I will not trust dreams to do what only a composed fable can do—convey wisdom by consistent allegory.

Talking with Millicent Dillon

This interview took place on 20 June 1977 in Davie's office on the Stanford University campus in Stanford, California.

Some years ago in a dispute with A. Alvarez you made a statement about decency in poetry and life. Speaking of the strain on human relations in the world we live in, you said, "One must make what efforts one can to relieve this pressure so that human relations may, as far as possible, be decent. One does this certainly, not by burdening the human relation with all the enormous weight of anxiety and responsibility which it seems to me you want to put on it."

Okay, why don't we start out from that point, the notion of taking the weight off relationships?

Yes . . . Well, what you have in mind is that passage from an interview which is seventeen years old. I was arguing with Alvarez, who in those days was the spokesman in England for the poetry and the suicide of Sylvia Plath, and for the poetry of Lowell and of John Berryman, which subsequently became "crowned," if that's the word, by suicide. Alvarez was irritated at that time by the refusal of British poets like me to use their writing as some sort of vehicle by which to let the public into the agonies of their personal relationships: the difficulties of their marriages, or with their children, or with their remembered parents. The implication of Alvarez, the interlocutor, was that *they* were obviously laying it on the line where we were not. I began my career at the time when Dylan Thomas's reputation was at its height. In the writing of Thomas and his imitators, one saw the blurring of the personal and private life of the poet as individual with the necessarily public life of the poet, as the latest instance of the poetic vocation. I objected to this blurring, as did other people who were associated with me in the early fifties in England. The same breakdown between public and private was there in Lowell and Berryman and Sylvia Plath, though it so happens that I think that Lowell and Berryman could write much better than Thomas and his disciples. And although we see less of it today, I think this is only an intermission. I think if readers were pressed, they would still say that the poet has a sort of duty to let down his hair in public, to undress in public, to let the reader into affairs which older generations would have regarded as private and intimate. This is bad, I believe, not only for art but for personal morality and human relations. If a marriage is shaky, then, it seems to me, the reaction to the situation should not be to frankly talk it out, to build up anxiety and demands upon the relationship. If the relationship is to survive at all, perhaps each of the partners has to put less weight upon it . . . discover other areas in which to enact some of their emotional needs. This is the way in which the majority of people have always acted in these situations and do still. I don't see why what holds for the majority of people who are not artists should not hold as well for people who are artists.

By that you don't mean to say that your own poetry is not personal—because your own poetry is personal, and you do write out of your own life, isn't that so?

Yes, indeed. Before now I have made a wordplay with four words: "private" and "public," "personal" and "impersonal." In lyric poetry—that's the clearest example, but to a degree in all sorts of writing—what you are doing is making the personal impersonal. This is different from making the private public. This is what T. S. Eliot meant, though he didn't put it properly in my view, in an essay that was very famous and influential through the years, about impersonality. I think what Eliot meant was that the process of creating a poem is to *depersonalize*. People don't understand that, I think, because he didn't put it clearly. Certainly a poem is no good if something personally rather difficult—personally rather discreditable—isn't near the heart of it. But then the business of art is to release and utter those painful or in many cases shameful things without embarrassing the person who hears you say them.

It's not sheerly a matter of embarrassment, is it? Doesn't it also have something to do with what can finally not be received by another human being in verse or in fiction if it is too direct? Do you see what I mean?

Yes, I think so. Embarrassment is too weak a word, actually.

Perhaps the forms and the conventions permit us to receive things by a side door, as it were, to be taken unawares by things that otherwise we would defend too much.

I think this is probably true, Millicent. I find it easier to define what we are talking about in terms of what it is not, rather than what it is. For instance, it cannot be right that the function of the reader of poetry is to live vicariously the extreme situations of the poet. This, it seems to me, is a profoundly discreditable transaction on both sides, and I've said this particularly in relation to Dylan Thomas, though it fits other famous cases. For the reader, this I think is very bad—indeed, very *squalid* (is that the word?)—where he is living through a suicidal state of mind, or living through alcoholism, or living through a ghastly tormented marriage, without himself taking any risks; the poet has taken them for him. And he then is getting feelings without having made any outlay for them. The reader certainly is not confronting what the poet is uttering to him. He is, as it were, grabbing it and running away with it. The poet is being used simply as the trigger for the reader to indulge, vicariously and cheaply, his own excitement.

In connection with this—I've told you this before—your criticism seems to me to be very direct and personal. Reading your critical essays, I get a much greater sense of a personal voice than I do when I read many other critics, in the United States at least. I think you once said something to me about this being partially a matter of the British versus the American convention.

It's true, there is a difference in the conventions. A degree of unbuttoned trenchancy, sharpness, a frank avowal of a personal reaction, is, I think, much more common in British reviewing than in American. I must say, though, that a degree of impatience, and perhaps excessive sharpness, is something that I'm aware of as growing upon me in the critical polemics that I find myself writing lately. Some people in England are offended or disconcerted by this, just as many American readers are. It could well be that this is bad strategy on my part, that my own impatience does nowadays appear in my criticism altogether too conspicuously. I think "impatience" is the word. After all, I've been active in the literary life of Britain and America now for more than a quarter of a century, and I *do* get impatient when I see people still mired in the same totally self-contradictory attitudes that they were in in 1948. I'm not excusing myself, but I think that if there is an increasingly brusque impatience in my critical writing, that is how I account for it. I also do think that time must be running out on us, that in 1977 we really must be operating with less time left to us than we were in 1947. The time I have in mind is the time before a total cultural breakdown. That sort of phrase is a very pompous one, and yet it has meaning for me. I really do think that we may very well foresee, before the end of the century, the end of what we have regarded as the standards of civilization, in human and social relations as well as in the forms of art. So I do get a feeling of crisis and emergency which translates itself into brusqueness and impatience in my criticism. One last point: you say that it is more there in the criticism than in the poetry. Well, this is because criticism is for me a second-order activity. I am just not prepared to take as much time in polishing and adjusting the tone of a book review as I am of a poem. And this has always been the case.

In the piece that you did on your West Riding boyhood, you talk about learning from your parents, particularly your mother, a great reverence for literature, and oddly just at the time literature was beginning to be treated with a kind of contempt, even by those who practiced it. You quoted one of the French poets . . .

Verlaine.

Yes. And then you spoke of your feeling that from the beginning you were starting with something that was almost lost. But maybe one doesn't really believe that one starts with something that is lost. . . .

That was an apprehension right at the edge of my youthful mind, whereas it is now, and has for many years been, quite central to me. Yes, the end of a civilization based upon the printed word. Now, I think it important to distinguish this from what we were talking about a few moments ago. I am perfectly willing to admit that you can have a very fine and valuable civilization in which the central modes of expression are not the printed word at all: a civilization built around—I don't know—sculpture or dance or music. It so happens that through my conditioning through my parents, civilization was from the first and has remained for me specifically a *literary* civilization.

I always have the sense that in your criticism you are defending, that you are guarding, though many people respond to you as if you were attacking.

It does follow in fact from what we have been saying that, yes, I do conceive of myself as fighting a delaying rearguard action. Well, it's got to be the case, hasn't it, in criticism, that you only attack what you think to be second-rate or dishonest for what you think to be honest and noble? Coleridge said this. It is the only vindication of criticism. Criticism must expose the false because if the false gets unchallenged currency, the first casualty will be the true. Every true poet is hindered if one of the innumerable false poets around him goes unexposed. This makes it sound, incidentally, as if my criticism is uniformly—what's the word?

Vitriolic.

Yes, as if I spend all my time cutting reputations down to size. There is quite a lot, but. . . .

Well, a number of pieces are like that, but not all of them certainly. The point I'm trying to make is that you seem to have a reputation that goes beyond what you actually say. People in the United States, for instance, receive your words as more of an attack than they really are. I think it's not just a matter of convention. What is it that makes it so hard for American readers to accept the criticism you write about and practice?

Actually this is a bit difficult because I'm the last person to know what my reputation is in the United States or anywhere. The majority of what passes for literary criticism, whether it's written in America or Britain or Australia, is done by people who are, by and large, amiable—not to say, timid—people. This is nothing novel and nothing particularly shameful. I would like to think that the sort of criticism that I have practiced or tried to practice is modeled upon an American critic, I mean Ezra Pound. And, of course, it's perfectly true that Pound's criticism does disconcert and sometimes enrage American as well as British readers. But it seems to me quite plain in Pound's career as a whole that he's brusque because of impatience, and he's impatient because of the things that he envisages British and American poetry doing, which they manifestly are not doing. I think he also is a profoundly generous critic, that he does attack the second raters only because he is determined to clear a space where the really good talents of his time become conspicuous and visible. And one thing that nobody denies about Pound is, in fact, the practical generosity of his concerns for his peers like Eliot and Joyce and Frost and D. H. Lawrence and Marianne Moore and William Carlos Williams. I would not say, I *could* not say, that I've been as generous as Pound was in actually giving time to advancing the claims of my contemporaries and rivals rather than advancing my own career—which is certainly what Pound did through long periods. But I have in fact done some championing of people who might otherwise have been considered my rivals. I would like to have done more. And I would like to think that when I knock other people, it is not because of personal hostility toward them or spite against them, but because I can see that if their defects are not recognized, then some other poet like them, but significantly different and better, is going to get obscured.

Do you tie this viewpoint of yours up in any way to your coming from a family that practiced religious dissent? Do you think that background had some effect on how you see yourself as guarding, or attacking to guard?

I would like to answer yes to this, Millicent, because one would always like to be able to put as much of one's life together as one can at any given moment. But I must say, I don't honestly think so. When I begin to kick it around in my head, there are analogies. The English dissenting or nonconformist churches are necessarily in tension with the established church, the Church of England. In that way, I suppose, it is true that an Englishman who was raised a dissenter, a Baptist, as I was, is preconditioned towards bucking the majority consensus. I can see this as an interesting theme to explore in an essay. I don't feel it as having worked that way in my case, though I can well see that it might. It's certainly very interesting, and to my surprise very little understood, that this is one of the crucial ways in which British experience differs from the American. An American Episcopalian is in communion with the Church of England, but there is of course no established church in this country. The Episcopalian church has no authority or priority beyond the Baptist, the Congregationalist, the Unitarian, the Presbyterian, and so on. And I think American readers are not very often made aware of this. That, however, I don't think has anything to do with my particular case, though it may have—it may. . . .

I was also thinking about the essay you wrote in My Cambridge. *There you mention coming to Cambridge as an outsider, not only as a boy from the North, but as a dissenter. Do you say "a dissenter" or "a young man from a dissenting family"?*

A young dissenter. "Nonconformist" is the word that is more often used in England, though I like "dissenter" more because it has more historical resonance. That's what they called themselves back in the seventeenth or eighteenth century.

This is a very interesting question to me, what that experience must have been like for you to come to Cambridge from the north as a dissenter, the kind of tensions you encountered and how you tried to reconcile them.

Raymond Williams, a good friend of mine, also contributed to that symposium of essays about Cambridge which you've been reading. Now Raymond's background is in many ways analogous to mine. I don't know about his religious background, but he certainly comes from a working-class family very far from the London-Oxford-Cambridge area, from a place, indeed, on the Welsh border. Like me he comes from a very, very—petty bourgeois I suppose is the word—a shopkeeper class, in the unfashionable provinces. He comes from the west; I come from the north. And yet the attitudes we take up, Williams and I, toward the metropolitan culture we were brought in contact with, are very different.

Your solution was to try to reconcile the two worlds, the one you'd come from and the new, the other one.

Yes. I think reconciliation is a good word. Whereas Raymond Williams seems to see it as a duty to hang on to the culture he had before he came to Cambridge, to protect that culture against the Cambridge culture, I don't feel that. The provincial culture and the metropolitan culture have to be reconciled. I believe they must be, and they can be. If "reconciliation" is the word for what one does in life and what one does in every poem that one writes, then it stands to reason that there have to be tensions that are to be reconciled and those tensions are not to be so totally reconciled that they actually disappear.

Now I want to ask you about a statement that you made about the Russian poets, about Mandelstam in particular, but I think it also applied to Pasternak. You said that because of the experience that they had with the Soviet regime they were able to speak of things in their poetry unselfconsciously, in a way that many poets in the United States and England cannot do. Do you still agree with that?

The Russian poets have always been important to me, but in a very peculiar way. This came about quite accidentally because it so happens that when I joined the Royal Navy in World War II the first posting that I got was to

north Russia where I spent eighteen months ashore work-
ing at wireless stations that we maintained there to guide
the convoys out around the North Cape. In Murmansk
and Archangel I learned the sort of disreputable Russian
that a sailor learns on shore leave, that's to say, very dis-
reputable in scholarly terms—never altogether serviceable
and yet just serviceable enough so that that language
was not totally closed to me. I also went there, you see,
when I was nineteen or twenty years old, at the most im-
pressionable period of one's life, when I was immensely
taken by the scope and scale and melancholy of the
Russian enterprise, the exoticism of the Russian char-
acter. It set me to reading a lot of Russian literature, as
much as I could get hold of for many years after that.
But my Russian was never good enough for me to be able
to read their poets with ease. I've always had to struggle
at a text with a dictionary and a grammar. But perhaps
that means that when I do engage with a Russian poet I
engage with him very closely indeed. I spend a lot of time
on it and I'm working over every word with the help of
a dictionary. So that, although my judgments on Russian
poets like Pushkin, Pasternak, Akhmatova, Mandelstam
are not trustworthy because I'm not at all inward enough
with the language, it is nevertheless a very intimate expe-
rience of them that I speak of. I do indeed regard the wit-
ness of the lives as well as the writings of those Russian
poets as a continual standard by which British and
American poets should measure themselves up more
often than they do. Now I say it's a standard by which
we should measure ourselves up. I do not say that they
are a standing reproach to us, you understand me. If
there are pressures in our societies to suppress and emas-
culate the sort of truth telling that poetry represents,
those pressures toward conformity and amenity are ob-
viously not only more devious but also much more
gentle. Let's face it: we are not going to be imprisoned

or sent to a mental home or sent to Siberia for anything that *we* write. We are not going to be prevented from publishing anything. I know also the argument that one used to hear a lot, a few years ago, which says that this is "repressive tolerance." It is perfectly true that a poet can find himself thinking, "I wish that the regime I lived under cared about what I do enough to suppress me." I don't trust that way of argument.

Russian poets like Pasternak and Mandelstam, with no doubt at all that their voices are in opposition to the organized consensus of their nation, are much less tempted than we are to go more than halfway to meet their public. In a curious way this *does* release them into recognizing the inherent value of their art as art. In their ways of saying what they want to say, they are drawing upon precedents and models and traditions which they are aware of, though the mass of their countrymen are not. This fact, which too often makes British and American poets feel guilty, makes them exultant.

As you said that, I thought of one of the earlier things we spoke about, of Dylan Thomas and how readers often used Thomas's private experience vicariously. For Mandelstam and Pasternak the experience they wrote out of was at one and the same time a deeply private and yet a political and public experience. So in their case poetry and action had different meanings with respect to each other—do you see what I mean?

I'm not sure if I'm addressing myself to what you have in mind, but I think Pasternak is a good case in point anyhow. What was it that the Soviet regime in the end could not abide about Pasternak? He hadn't deliberately flouted their conventions. He hadn't explicitly and consistently attacked their assumptions in the way that

Solzhenitsyn did or to some degree even Mandelstam did. Pasternak was much of the time genuinely a guy who wanted to accommodate so far as he could, yet in the end he too could not avoid explicit confrontation. Why? Because he was asserting the worth and the autonomy of the private life of human relations in a society in which everything is public, in which there are no human and personal relations that are not also social relations. That is all, as far as I can see, that Pasternak is implicitly asserting in his poems and indeed in *Dr. Zhivago*. Thus the most politically outrageous thing you can say in a thoroughly socialized and totalitarian state is that a great deal of my most valuable and important life which I want to share with other people is life which is lived in private. What's shocking, of course, is that we, living in societies in which it is still possible for that fruitful tension between the private and the public, the personal and the impersonal, to be maintained, all too many of us, apparently, want to destroy it. We too, under no compulsion at all, seem to want to make the private public, want to undress in public, want to destroy the possibility of privacy. Under an achieved socialized totalitarian state there is explicit pressure to do that. On us there is some pressure, but very little. Yet some of us, and self-styled artists particularly, are all too ready to do it for ourselves. But now I am getting brusque and impatient again.

Talking about brusqueness and impatience—let's go to the essay on art and anger. In that essay which you originally wrote in 1970 and then added to in 1977, you are talking about the question of right anger in art, about what is rancor and what is destructive anger. You say something about connections between the act of writing a poem and acts of irrational violence. At the same time, I remember one sentence from your essay in My Cambridge, *in which you talked about going to Russia as a young man and becoming aware of certain anarchic things within yourself, of the irrational within yourself. Maybe you could talk a little about the appeal of irrational violence and the reconciliation of it in your own poetry.*

That essay about art and anger, as I say in the text, was originally delivered at a conference at the University of California at Irvine. In order to start us off, the sponsors proposed certain things. One of their propositions was that there was a relationship between irrational violence and the act of making a poem. In the text I say that I deny that relationship. You're asking me to think again about that, particularly since you rightly have noticed that in at least one place, I admit propensities towards anarchic and violent behavior in myself . . . . Well, I suppose I can only answer this out of prejudice. The people who are readiest to tolerate or apologize for anarchic violence in others, and who are most excited by creating it or responding to it in literature, are in my experience people who live at a very low emotional temperature. If it's paradoxical, it's a very obvious and easy paradox. The person who is most afraid of anarchic or violent propensities in others is most aware of them in himself. If you are in fact not naturally a violent person, then violence comes as a spice, as an interesting and exotic phenomenon which you can experience through observing the actions of others, or by participating in mass actions, or by getting it vicariously through literature. But if you are a person who knows that you have anarchic, subversive, and violent potentialities in yourself, then you know these demons all too well and you are very concerned not to give them their head in your own behavior, nor to incite them in the behavior of others. In that sense, the calm, the harmony, the reconciliation which a poem aims at—and if it's successful, achieves—is motivated by the something that has to be controlled, harmonized, and pacified: our impulse towards irrational violence. I find it easiest here to think of a particular case, Dr. Samuel Johnson, who is a great apostle in his own writing and in his criticism of order, sanity, and harmony. And yet we know from his biographer that he was a profoundly neurotic man, a man who was hounded by nightmares. We have evidence of this in his prayers and meditations and the way he would wake up his friends in the night because he couldn't last any longer without company. This relationship between violence and order can be played either way. On the one hand, it is possible to say, as people do say who do not care for Dr. Johnson, that Johnson was neurotic and compulsive and had nightmares, precisely because he would not release the spontaneous anarchic violent propensities in himself. That is one way of arguing it. I would always argue it the other way around. The order, the harmony which he achieved in his life as well as in his art is valuable and exemplary precisely because there was in him a great deal to be harmonized and ordered, with great difficulty. This really is just returning full circle on that question about reconciliation of tensions.

I'll take one other question out of this same essay. Speaking of revolution, you say, "The poet has too much stake in the inheritance, first and foremost in that inheritance which is his language, to lend himself to that sort of fresh start. He cannot imagine it, and it is his duty that as against the philosopher, for instance, what he cannot imagine he will not conceive." I'm curious as to what your notion of the imagination is as opposed to the notion of what conception is.

There's an anecdote which has been repeated so many times that it's hackneyed, but it's still very useful. Renoir, the painter, said to Mallarmé the poet, "You know, I have a lot of ideas that I would like to put into poems." And Mallarmé said, "Poems are not written with ideas but with words." It is obviously not the case that *idea*, in the sense of conceptualizing, is the basic thing that goes on in a man or a woman who is writing a poem. If that is what you have, you have a string of logical propositions and concepts, which you want to communicate, and then obviously the conventions of verse are the merest foolish obstruction. They're not a rational way of going about it at all. People do not write philosophical nor theological, ideological treatises in verse. They used to do so in long past centuries, and very boring those works now are. So plainly we're not doing that. "Idea" is not what we are principally concerned with. In the sense that a painter's medium is paint, what is a poet's medium? Not ideas, but words, language. More of language is concerned with images than with ideas. Hence if I have an idea of something, I can conceive of it. But if I can't somehow clothe it in a form which is sensuously apprehensible, then, okay, I can use it in conversation or I can use it in a critical essay, but I can't use it in poems.

The reason I ask you this question is that in an essay in Agenda, *Martin Dodsworth quotes something you wrote about generalization. I think you said, "My mind moves most easily and happily among abstractions. It relates ideas far more readily than it relates experiences." Now this is putting you in kind of a tough place, Donald, but one of the things that may be in operation in terms of the development of your poetry is a tension between experience and conceptualization, parallel to that tension between your dissenting background and Cambridge.*

What you quote there, and what Martin Dodsworth quotes, is something that I dug out of an old notebook and put in the back of my *Collected Poems*. It's a specific journal entry which I wrote sometime in the middle 1950s, a good twenty years ago. It was the way I saw myself then. It has the sort of truth a testimony of a person about himself at a given moment has. Let's put it this way: in order to get myself from my provincial backwater near to something like the center, in terms of clusterings and monuments of my culture, I had to use the educational system. I had to get very good at working up through that educational system. Now the educational system of Britain in the 1930s was, and I suppose still is insofar as it survives, an education based upon the "idea," the capacity to formulate ideas, handle them, and string them together. Therefore it is perfectly true to say that I was trained, I trained myself, in the handling of ideas and abstractions—never, I may say, with the extreme conceptual abstraction that we associate with either the mathematician or the philosopher. I never had training of that sort and I'm no sort of a philosopher at all; I can't read it mostly. But still, the sort of ideas you have in order to write an essay about politics or the relationship of culture and society, that sort of handling of ideas I trained myself in—my education trained me in— and I got good at it. And because I got good at it, I got where I wanted to go. But it is perfectly true that when I wanted to write poems I did have to consciously unlearn a great deal of those skills and disciplines which had got me where I was. And it was by studying Pasternak particularly, very intensely in the late 1950s and the 1960s, that I learned how to suppress the abstracting and conceptualizing part of my intelligence in favor of the image-making and sensuous perceptions.

There was one other thing in that essay which puzzled me—your use of the word contempt there.

Oh, yes.

You said that in Yeats and Pope the anger is more than half contempt. "This has to be, so that the anger is cleanly and completely discharged." For somebody like you who is always putting such emphasis upon the necessity of decency in the relationship between people and between reader and writer, I was surprised by the notion of contempt. In this case it seemed to me you used it in a positive sense.

Yes, that worries me too. It followed from my argument at that point in the "Art and Anger" piece. It still seems to be true about both Yeats and Pope, whom I offer as splendid examples of the cleanness and clarity of anger in art. And yet I am uneasy, as you rightly suppose, at having got myself into the position of taking something like contempt and giving it a sort of positive charge. In fact, since I wrote that, in the last several weeks I've been reading a French sociologist called Jacques Ellul, one of my current enthusiasms, who made me very uncomfortable when he defined the present age as an age of scorn and derision. And when I read that I paused, and I remembered those sentences in "Art and Anger," and I was very, very troubled. I suppose at this point all I should say is I'm still troubled.

Let me ask you two more questions. In the last line of the piece on Lowell that you did for the New York Times Book Review, *you ask how seriously do we take what a poet or a poem says. Do you want to take some time to speak about that?*

Yes. These are the hardest questions that you've kept for the end. I suppose it's strategy.

Well, we were warming up on the others.

It isn't an easy one, Millicent, if only, for heaven's sake, because this is precisely the question that's been debated since ancient Greece, in every generation. What is the status of the statements that the poet makes in his poem? Are they, as I. A. Richards said sixty years ago, pseudo-statements? Are they not to be taken as verifiable in a way in which other statements made in science or in ordinary human intercourse are to be taken? To take that line that Richards offers there solves a lot of the difficulties. And yet I'm very reluctant to take that line. It is obvious in one sense that the statements which a poet makes in his poems are not statements we associate with other areas of discourse. "My love is like a red red rose," says Robert Burns, and plainly you are not supposed to say, "Oh yes, how? Has she got a high color? Has she got thorns?" In that sense it is true that poetry is often making statements which are logically nonsense. On the other hand, while accepting that, I do not see why a poet in a poem should be absolved from the duty which we lay on ourselves and on others in other walks of life, of meaning what he says, of saying things which he will stand by. Once we accept that a poet is absolved from that duty which bears upon the rest of us, then what is left for poetry except to be a curious entrancing murmur in the background? Again I think of the martyrs and heroes of poetry in our time, the Russian poets, particularly. To take that view of poetry is surely to insult the memory of the Akhmatovas and Mandelstams and Pasternaks. When a poet makes a statement in a poem he should be held not less responsible but more responsible than he is when he makes statements in a lecture or in an interview. The particular point at issue in the Lowell is of course very, very difficult indeed and I admit then and there that it's an insoluble one. What happens when a poet changes his mind? What happens when a poet who was a Communist sincerely, and sincerely expressed his Communism in poems that he wrote in 1935, has ceased to believe in it by the time he comes to collect those poems for his collected edition thirty years later? Well, this was the problem with W. H. Auden. Auden solved it in one way by eliminating all those pro-Communist statements he'd made. As I say in the essay, that doesn't seem to be quite right either. Yet one can honor the single-mindedness in Auden that led him to do that. I'm not aware of having said anything on any page of my collected poems which I did not mean then and do not mean now. If I came across a case of a statement which I duly meant when I wrote it then, but no longer could say now, I'd be in a very curious state and I don't know what I'd do.

One last question, about "In the Stopping Train." You once talked about it as a poem about yourself and your alter ego. Do you want to say something about that poem and its statement, about the question of the balance between meaning and feeling, between language and experience? You don't have the feeling that talking about it will negate the poem in any way?

Not if I say only a little .... You start by asking about the alter ego in the poem. It's true that the basic device is to set up an "I" and a "he," to split myself in two. This is not to be taken as meaning that in any way it was written in a schizoid frame of mind or that in any way it is an exploration of potential schizophrenia. It was in fact a deliberate device to effect that which we started this interview by talking about, to effect the de-personalizing of a highly personal theme. Thom Gunn, my good friend, was very quick to realize this, as I would expect a fellow poet to be. "In the Stopping Train" is nearly a "confessional" poem—that's an unsatisfactory term, but it's one that's been around. As I said, I don't like confessional poems in the sense of poems which make the private public while not depersonalizing it. I try to depersonalize by the very simple device of changing the first person into the third and talking about myself, some of the time, as if I were a third person, a "he." The poem is an expression of a mood of profound depression and uncertainty about what it has meant for me person-ally, and for people close to me, that for so many years I have devoted myself to this curious activity we call po-etry. It explores the possibility that what we call poetry, poetry writing, is a will-o'-the-wisp—if not something worse, an egotistical self-indulgence. And, in fact, the poem, like any poem, because it's dealing with images and not with ideas, doesn't argue whether this is so or not. In its various sections it expresses the experience of feeling that way, having doubts, and a degree of self-disgust about the whole business. At some point these doubts have to do with the relationship between language and experience. You write a poem and you string a lot of language together and you think, or you deceive your-self, that by stringing language together you're somehow putting in a meaningful pattern the experiences which those words stand for. But what if you're not doing anything of the sort? What if, in fact, you never break out of a verbal world into a world of the things named, if you never get from names to the things named? My example in that poem is flowers. I'm very bad at flowers. I never go into gardens. Oh, I mean I go into gardens, but I never garden. My wife does. I know the names of flowers but I can't recognize very many. This is disconcerting. I use those names of flowers in poems because poems are made of words or names. And yet, isn't it very odd that I can use a word like valerian and yet wouldn't know a valerian if I saw one? And I would have thought that no poet is any good, or can probe very far, if he doesn't have periods in his life at which this sort of quite disabling doubt about the value of the whole activity doesn't come to him.

Go Home, Octavio Paz!

Go home, Octavio Paz! And go home also, Neruda, Yves Bonnefoy, Hans Magnus Enzensburger, Ungaretti, Bella Akhmadulina, Anthony Hecht. Go home, every good poet who has been lured to London this week for Poetry International '67.

If it is too late for them to stay home, as Voznesensky and Yevtushenko have done, let them take a leaf out of Charles Olson's book, and hop a plane at once. They have been brought here under false pretenses.

For after all, how can foreign poets know what it means to be introduced by Malcolm Muggeridge, as they may be for five nights this week in the Royal Festival Hall? Mr. Muggeridge, impudently aboveboard as ever, knows perfectly well what it means and makes no secret of his knowledge. This very week he puts on record his opinion of T. S. Eliot: "Eliot was the biggest phony of all, the death rattle in the throat of a dying civilization." These are the opinions, and this is the language, with which to associate Giuseppe Ungaretti? What refined insolence to think so, and what an ingenious trick to play on that octogenarian poet, to smear him with these associations without his knowing it! We begin to see how this

---

This article first appeared in the *Guardian*, July 1967.

was one charade Mr. Muggeridge could not be left out of. And how he must relish the exquisite imbecilities of some of Poetry International's organizers—of Mr. Patrick Garland telling the *London Times* he would "almost break a leg to hear a great poet reading his own works," because, even if he is reading in a language Mr. Garland doesn't know, that's all right, since "it doesn't matter how eccentrically he reads, or whether one understands what it's all about. It's the rhythm that counts."

With what delight, as a connoisseur of British absurdity, Malcolm Muggeridge may set this beside Ted Hughes's declaration that poetry is "a universal language of understanding, coherent behind the many languages, in which we can all hope to meet." (It's the rhythm that counts.)

No, Mr. Muggeridge's interest in these goings-on is plain. It is in keeping with the startlingly consistent role he has defined for himself these last years—of assisting sardonically and positively, and yet with complete lucidity, at the steady spray of infection from London over every center of what was once civilization. And the cream of the joke is that it's an in-joke: these distinguished foreigners will not know what they are assisting at; they would be appalled.

The Americans, it may be thought, should have found out some time ago. And perhaps some of them have. The latest information is that Anne Sexton, for instance, is absenting herself. I'm delighted to hear it. And I'm even more delighted to see that Robert Lowell apparently would have no part in this nonsense from the start. How could he, in view of the hardly less conspicuous absence of British poets he is known to admire, such as Betjeman and Larkin? But there are plenty of British faces to adorn the sorry spectacle—Empson and Graves, alas, and Stephen Spender of course, and Hugh

MacDiarmid and Patrick Kavanagh. Perhaps it is not too late to urge them also to have second thoughts, to look at the publicity that has been put out, and to ask themselves in all seriousness whether anything can come out of such vulgar nonsense except what is harmful to poetry as they have known and practiced it; whether, in particular, that "great and growing public for poetry" which Ted Hughes tries to conjure into existence in London by asserting that it exists already, isn't in fact an audience for irrationality and mass hysteria.

Hughes and Garland, I am willing to believe, are acting from the highest motives. But Hughes is the author of a handout which fervently and wishfully contradicts every reality that a levelheaded man can recognize about our present world, and the place of poetry in that world. And poetry is contemptible if it can defy reality only by denying it.

The *Times Literary Supplement* has declared: "Certainly it will be a grim comment on our culture if there are any empty seats in the Queen Elizabeth Hall next week." On the contrary it will be wonderful if the hall is empty every night of the five. But this is too much to hope for. Let the seats in the hall be filled, and the seats on the platform empty.

Art and Anger

On 21 and 22 May 1970, the Program in Creative Writing of the University of California at Irvine, together with the graduate division of the Department of English there, sponsored a conference under the rubric, "Art and Anger." In the leaflet which the sponsors distributed to participants, they declared:

> This conference will explore the connections between literature and social upheaval: between the act of writing a poem and acts of irrational violence. Connections run deep. The poet has a stake in the irrational, in the forces which both create poetry and destroy social order; the poet also has a stake in preserving social order and his cultural heritage. The violence of social and psychological change may provoke his Muse to descend and stimulate him to write; but his language, his form, and his entire mode of expression derive from culture. He knows that culture and social order exist by virtue of repression; he also knows that the poet breaks through repression. Hence a dilemma: a challenging set of paradoxes.

I began my contribution by quoting famous verses from the Second Dialogue of Alexander Pope's "Epilogue to the Satires" (1738):

> Ask you what provocation I have had?
> The strong Antipathy of Good to Bad.

When Truth or Virtue an Affront endures,
Th'Affront is mine, my friend, and should be yours.
Mine as Foe profess'd to false Pretence,
Who thinks a Coxcomb's Honour like his sense;
Mine, as a Friend to ev'ry worthy mind;
And mine as Man, who feel for all mankind.
   F. You're strangely proud.
          P. So proud, I am no Slave:
So impudent, I own myself no Knave:
So odd, my Country's Ruin makes me grave.
Yes, I am proud; I must be proud to see
Men not afraid of God, afraid of me:
Safe from the Bar, the Pulpit, and the Throne,
Yet touch'd and sham'd by Ridicule alone.

Anger? Surely. And "art"? Superbly; though the anger can afford to be thus superbly explicit only because (1) this is an old and famous poet justly calling upon the evidence of a lifetime's witness to the social responsibility of himself as poet; and (2) he writes in and for an age in which fear of God was a religious duty constantly inculcated and immediately experienced (so that what looks like pride, and declares itself such, is really humility, in that it is only the utterly depraved, the merest scum of society, who—since God's wrath cannot touch them— may be stung by that less than God-like thing, a poet).

But if this is my touchstone of the relation between Art and Anger at its most splendid and admirably fruitful, I'm at a loss to know how to get from this to what (it seems) we are expected to discuss under this rubric; "the connections . . . between the act of writing a poem and acts of irrational violence." *I deny that any such connections exist*; and if Pope's lines may represent angry art at its most splendid and most moving, they move me away from rather than towards any sympathy with "acts of irrational violence."

Again, it is suggested to us that "the poet has a stake in the irrational, in the forces which both create poetry and destroy social order; the poet also has a stake in preserving social order and his cultural heritage." Still going by Alexander Pope as my mentor and exemplar, *I deny the first stake, and affirm the second*. For Pope's anger—preeminently in the *Dunciad*, but consistently throughout his career—was directed against those who threatened social order and would squander the cultural heritage—and indeed it is his consistent tenacity in directing his anger always (as he saw it) at these targets, which makes his lifelong anger heroic. (To be sure, when we speak of "social order" in this case, we do not mean the law and order of the current political "Establishment." For in the poems from which I've quoted, as in others for twenty years before, Pope's main target is the effective first executive of the English state, the king's first minister, Robert Walpole. The head of state may be the worst enemy of social order in that state—as some people believe is the case in the United States at the present day [1970]. All the same, the poet's anger is on behalf of order and against disorder—even, or especially, when the worst fomenter of disorder is the man who should be keeping order.)

Let me jump ahead at once to the hardest of the sayings which come to me from this example of angry art, and from others which come to mind—that the act of poetry is by necessity and of its nature in the profoundest sense *conservative*. Or—to reverse the proposition and make it more challenging still—that a revolutionary poet is a contradiction in terms. (When Pound and Yeats ceased to be conservatives and spoke as revolutionaries, they turned out to be revolutionaries of the right, i.e., fascists. They damaged their art and betrayed their vocation.)

The poet, we are reminded, knows that "his language, his form, and his entire mode of expression derive from culture." Yes, indeed! And revolution, as we have known it in our century (as distinct from what the Americans knew in 1776 or even the French in 1790), is not a bid to revitalize and redirect the inherited culture, but a bid to cancel it out, to obliterate it or rule it out as irrelevant, and to start *afresh*. And the poet has too much stake in the inheritance—first and foremost, in that inheritance which is his language—to lend himself to that sort of "fresh" start. He cannot imagine it; and it is his duty that—as against the philosopher, for instance—what he cannot imagine, he will not conceive.

But I'm more interested in trying to distinguish anger from other manifestations that are often confused with it, and from which indeed (in the case of particular works of art) it is hard to distinguish it. I have in mind, in the first place, *hatred*, *rancor*, and *indignation*. Anger, I believe (and may even say that I know from experience), nourishes art; it makes for a clean discharge of emotional energy, articulately. Hatred and rancor, on the other hand, are "a slow burn"—the man who experiences them learns to live with them, grows habituated to them, grows to need them and to depend on them, to like these feelings and to luxuriate in them. Accordingly hatred and rancor do not impel a person to discharge his feelings in act or in the poet's act of speech. They nourish neither action nor art; instead they nurse themselves, stoke their own fires; they are inward-turning, self-regarding, and self-nourishing; the last thing they want is to be discharged. Accordingly I take hatred and rancor to be profoundly and essentially antiartistic. And the point is worth emphasizing because lots of people plume themselves on feeling anger when what they are really feeling is a sterile hatred or a mean rancor. And here I may be allowed to speak with some special and mournful authority, as an Englishman—i.e., as citizen of a country where class hatred, under the specious disguise of class solidarity, is daily offered as a civic virtue and a social duty. As for *indignation*, though I bow to the traditional ascription of *saeva indignatio* to the time-honored form of Juvenalian satire, and accordingly I am sure that indignation can nourish art and action as anger can, yet I believe that as indignation is directed more at actions, policies, and institutions than at persons (as anger is), indignation is, even more than anger, liable to be confounded with the sterile emotions of rancor and hatred.

Indignation, like anger, is a flash point, not a slow burn like rancor. But, unlike anger, indignation can always find occasions. And I would ask in all sincerity of those who share my indignation at the invasion of Cambodia whether the feeling of righteous indignation which we experience (however righteous, however just) isn't in the long run *luxurious*. How simple life is, when we have, and know we must keep as a political duty, feelings of indignation and outrage! In such a psychological situation, how much that is ultimately more baffling and ambiguous in our mental lives can be disregarded or suppressed or put on the back burner! Once we've experienced this blessedly simplified state, don't we feel the temptation to prolong the condition, pharisaically seeking out other things to be indignant about? It is a hard thing to acknowledge; but we can get to like our indignations, and to rely on them as on a drug. The artist has the duty to resist such seductive simplifications of his mental and emotional life; and to insist that human consciousness, though it comprehends political consciousness, transcends it. The only poem that I know which deals with this issue, glancingly, is a British poem by Kingsley Amis, "After Goliath."

SECOND THOUGHTS (1977)

To take up this subject after seven years is to recognize with a shock what a difference those years have made. In 1970, under the Nixon presidency, as the United States was brutally and precipitately extricating itself from the ruins of its intervention in Southeast Asia, the connection between art and anger was of immediate concern for American poets and many of their American readers; because poems of "protest"—against the national policy, or else (more rarely) in support of that policy against internal protesters and dissidents—were in many cases the only poems that responsible poets felt able to write, or justified in writing. Seven years later it is as if that climate of sentiment had never been; and once again it is easy for people to suppose that anger never feeds art, or that it does so very seldom—in which case "Art and Anger" will seem to be an out-of-the-way topic, of (as they say) mainly academic interest.

However, I don't find it so—if only because the angers that I feel are prompted, as they always were, by the United Kingdom, rather than the United States; in particular by the arrogant rationalism and authoritarianism of British socialism, which is even more menacing and disgraceful in 1977 than it was in 1970. (Not that the distinction need be pressed very far; as words like "rationalism" and "arrogant" may suggest, the temper of mind of British administrators is at bottom the same as what affronted Americans in the slide-rule planners and strategists who forced them deeper and deeper into the bog of Vietnam.) Of the poems I have written since 1970 not many, but a few, have been fed by anger; and my British readers seem to resist and resent such poems even more than they used to do. I can't pretend to be surprised that what I take to be anger and indignation is interpreted by them as rancor and resentment; but at all events the matter for me isn't "academic" at all, but as compelling now as it was in 1970.

At the end of the first book of his *Philosophical Inquiry into the Origin of our Ideas of the Sublime and Beautiful*, Edmund Burke, having discoursed on Joy and Grief and Fear and Love and one or two other passions, decides that these are "almost the only ones which it can be necessary to consider," the only ones worthy "of an attentive investigation." It is surprising and it must be significant that, writing so soon as he did after the death of Pope, a great poet of anger, Burke neither at this point nor elsewhere in his treatise considers among the passions either anger or indignation. If we look in his pages for any acknowledgment of the effect made on us by

> Yes, I am proud; I must be proud to see
> Men not afraid of God, afraid of me

we come nearest to it at 1, xvii, when Burke says:

> Hence proceeds what Longinus has observed of that glory-ing sense of inward greatness, that always fills the reader of such passages in poets and orators as are sublime.

But the connection is accidental and illusory, for Burke and Longinus are speaking of a sentiment aroused in the reader, not of a sentiment avowed by the poet, as Pope avows it here. And indeed there can be little doubt that Burke would have concurred with his contemporaries—with Thomas Warton, and with even so great an admirer of Pope as Dr. Johnson—in denying to Pope any touch of "the sublime." This would be inevitable, given Pope's clarity and on the other hand Burke's insistence that "the sublime" abhors clarity, being at home rather in the indistinct and the murky.

It was this in Burke that provoked another great poet of anger, William Blake, to explode in the margin of his copy of Reynolds's *Discourses*: "Obscurity is Neither the Source of the Sublime nor of anything Else." I am sure that Blake was right, and indeed I would say that because of its insistence to the contrary Burke's *Philosophical Inquiry* is, unintentionally, one of the most mischievous books ever written by a man of genius.

This will raise a smile. Isn't Burke's treatise merely a historical curiosity, which none of us needs to get heated about? I think not; though there are parts of it, notably book four, which indeed are now merely quaint, most of the time Burke is articulating mistaken ideas which have done vast damage ever since his time, and are rampant today. If "sublime" and "beautiful" are terms that we no longer find much use for, the reason is, I suspect, that in our apprehension of the arts—at any rate, of literature—what Burke called "the sublime" has long ago overborne "the beautiful." For us the beautiful means the pretty, the graceful, and the effeminate—a disastrous scaling down such as Burke in his book is quite manifestly (and, one must suppose, consciously) instigating or promoting. In a famous passage, where Burke is extolling sublimity in a passage from Milton, who is for him consistently and preeminently the English master of "the sublime," he writes:

The mind is hurried out of itself, by a crowd of great and confused images; which affect because they are crowded and confused. For, separate them, and you lose much of the greatness; and join them, and you infallibly lose the clearness. The images raised by poetry are always of this obscure kind.

And in another passage, following his ancient authority Longinus in going for sublimity to the Hebrew scriptures, Burke comments on some verses from the Book of Job:

> We are first prepared with the utmost solemnity for the vision; we are first terrified, before we are let even into the obscure cause of our emotion; but when the grand cause of terror makes its appearance, what is it? Is it not wrapt up in the shades of its own incomprehensible darkness, more awful, more striking, more terrible, than the liveliest description, than the clearest painting, could possibly represent it?

Take these two passages together, and do they not express what we experience—and what our children are glad to experience—in reading the *Ariel* poems of Sylvia Plath? There the poet is clearly expressing some vast dissatisfaction with herself and the terms of her life. But if that is clear, nothing else is. Plainly the *Ariel* poems are somehow angry poems; but what occasions the anger, what the anger is directed at—this is never clear. This possibility is mooted, and then another one, and then another, "a crowd of great and confused ideas." And apparently we like it that way; this is the sublime, and the sublime is what we like. What is plain is that a Plath poem is not, either for the poet or her readers, a clean discharge of the angry energies that went into its making. The poet pathetically admitted as much by killing herself. And so what emerges from the poems is ultimately *not* anger, but rancor, the slow burn, the gas oven. And surely the same is true of that other suicide, a far more winning and inventive writer, the late John Berryman; with Berryman too, it was the inability to focus his angers, to locate them, define them, and discharge them, which won him readers and compelled his suicide. He too in his jokey way "affected the sublime," and was esteemed by a public that despised beauty but was entertained by the sublime—all the more of a thrill if it claimed the life of the entertainer. The sublime, it turns out, is murkier than Edmund Burke could know. Disaffection, resentment, acedia, malaise, "alienation"—all those fashionable conditions, precisely because in all of them the sufferer "doesn't know what is wrong with him," produce in art "the sublime." Anger, on the other hand, and indignation, because they drive towards clarity and depend upon achieving it, belong in the other category, "the beautiful."

With the indistinct duplicities of a Plath or a Berryman, compare the clarity of an epigram by Yeats:

> Parnell came down the road, he said to a cheering man:
> 'Ireland shall get her freedom and you still break stone'.

That is the note of:

> Yes, I am proud; I must be proud to see
> Men not afraid of God, afraid of me.

And it is surely obvious why Yeats and Pope raise the modern reader's hackles, as Plath and Berryman don't. In Yeats and Pope the anger is more than half contempt. This has to be so, if the anger is to be cleanly and completely discharged; the occasion of the anger is consumed clean away, never to be thought of again. We may contrast a greater poet than Plath or Berryman, Yeats's friend Ezra Pound. Throughout the *Cantos* what is felt for Roosevelt and the Jews is never, strictly speaking, anger; the emotion never is, nor could it be, discharged—because the malefactions alleged against them are never focused with clarity, but come to us only as "a crowd of great and confused ideas." We speak only loosely and

61

misleadingly if we say that what Pound feels for Franklin Delano Roosevelt or Sir Basil Zaharoff is anger and contempt. If that were really what he felt, his hostility toward them would not rankle as it does through more than one hundred cantos and more than forty years. The *Cantos* are perhaps, or this side of them is, sublime; it cannot be beautiful. And my impression is that even by Jews and American Social Democrats Pound will be forgiven sooner than Yeats or Pope will—because the sublime is self-confessed muddle, and thereby democratic, whereas what Yeats and Pope feel and express is, along with anger, contempt. And in democracies contempt is unforgivable, as ultimately hatred isn't.

When Burke's friend Dr. Johnson, more than twenty years after the *Philosophical Inquiry*, undertook to write a life of Pope, he did not principally see Pope as a poet of anger. And indeed many other passions besides anger nourished Pope's art. Nevertheless, as Jean Hagstrum showed us long ago, Johnson's polemical endeavor through that one of his *Lives of the Poets* was to present Pope as throughout a poet of "the beautiful," without "the sublime" and "the pathetic" and yet no worse for lacking them. This is the true meaning of Johnson's famous rhetorical question: "If Pope be not a poet, where is poetry to be found?" And if for us Pope is far more conspicuously a poet of anger than he was for Johnson, none the less Johnson's argument holds good. Anger is beautiful; and the art that anger feeds is crisp and clear and bright, not the hulking and nebulous immensities of "the sublime."

The Life of Dylan Thomas

Dylan Thomas, the Anglo-Welsh poet, died of his excesses in 1953. I can't be impartial about him, though I never met him. The sort of poetry that he wrote, the taste in poetry that he appealed to and confirmed, above all the notions created by his notorious and disastrous career as to what is a normal relation between a poet and his public—these I had to struggle with when I began writing poems, and they obstruct me still, just as they obstruct (and in too many cases have destroyed) my contemporaries. The late John Berryman and the late Anne Sexton are just two poets who might, I believe, have had longer and happier lives if they hadn't grown up under the shadow of the Dylan legend.

If I'm not impartial, neither of course is Andrew Sinclair, who confesses to a "lifelong obsession with Dylan," who at one time was commissioned by the Dylan Thomas literary executors, and who plainly means to prejudice the issue by the subtitle of his book, *Dylan Thomas: No Man More Magical.* Fair's fair, however. Sinclair has written a much more responsible book than its format and its blurbs seem meant to suggest; and I

This article first appeared in the *New York Times Book Review*, 9 November 1975. © 1975/76 by The New York Times Company. Reprinted by permission.

imagine many a reader, seduced by the glossy photographs and, on the dust jacket, "the best lyric poet of his age ... the greatest lyric poet of his age," will feel cheated by Sinclair's mostly sober and judicious narrative. He supplies no colorful roustabout anecdotes and delivers instead such chastening judgments as "he was a poet of the villa and the family," or, "if his role of the *enfant terrible* was false, yet he played it to its death and his own." In fact, Sinclair is in some ways altogether too circumspect; because he sets his sights so consistently on Thomas as a private and domestic person, we are supposed to know for ourselves about Thomas's unparalleled fame—when it started, how it grew, who helped it along, who exploited it. Firmly insisting that in the end Thomas's self-destruction can be blamed on no one but Thomas himself, Sinclair rightly resists the sentimentalists who would have it that the poet was "a victim." And yet he could still have named the names of those who connived at the self-destruction, accelerated it, and made show biz money out of it. By not acknowledging how it was Thomas's fame that enabled him to destroy himself, Sinclair cannot deal with what, it seems to me, is the permanent lesson of Thomas's life story—that is to say, what it can mean nowadays for a poet to be famous and popular. His readers, acting out a vulgarized parody of the romantic idea of the poet as scapegoat, live out vicariously through him all the risks and excesses which they are too timid or prudent to live out for themselves; and they demand that in the end the poet pay—for their fantasies as well as for his own actions—by suicide.

If we ask what "lyric" means when Thomas is called, as he is by Sinclair, "the greatest lyric poet of his time" (in any language, apparently), the answer seems to be just what I've been spelling out: a lyric poet is one who is absolved from all civic responsibilities and all moral restraints on the strict understanding that by enacting his own self-destruction under the spotlights he shall vindicate his public in its resentful acquiescence to the restraints he is absolved from. Thomas would have followed out this logic easily enough; he was very sharp and unsparing in these matters, as we see whenever Sinclair quotes from his letters and reviews. Indeed, the horror is that Thomas almost certainly knew what was happening to him, even as he went along with it. Sinclair doesn't deny this, but he doesn't bring it out very forcibly.

Probably most people believe, as Andrew Sinclair seems to, that the squalid waste of the life is justified by the handful of poems which that life, and by implication that way of life, made possible. Reasonably enough, in what is a biography not a critical study, Sinclair takes it for granted that the artistic excellence of that handful of poems is universally admitted. It is not. Thomas's gifts were very great; but he used them to achieve effects which are, though powerful, artistically *coarse*. A taste for them is a taste that cannot respond to the subtleties and delicacies of the best of Thomas's forerunners and contemporaries. And there's evidence that Thomas knew that too. This much we can salute in him—he may have fooled others; he didn't fool himself.

John Berryman's
Freedom of the Poet

In J. D. O'Hara's picture book, *A History of Poetry*
1975), there appears a familiar photograph of the aging
John Berryman, with gurulike beard, flowing, grizzled,
unkempt. On the same page are pictures of Robert
Lowell, Sylvia Plath and Anne Sexton; and to all of these
the caption reads: "Lowell . . . was the first American
poet to write in the intimate, introspective verse style
that has since been dubbed 'confessional' poetry. This
new approach to poetry was to prove the undoing of at
least one of Lowell's contemporaries and two of his
disciples." And in case we have any doubt who the con-
temporary is, and who the disciples, the caption makes
it plain: "John Berryman . . . along with Sylvia Plath . . .
and Anne Sexton . . . , all harboring unresolved personal
torments, wrote poems filled with angst and death wishes
that were ultimately fulfilled by suicide." Perhaps un-
intentionally, this conveys the clear impression that
Berryman was a confused character who lost his head—
as did, more excusably, a couple of much younger poets—
because of the example of a stronger poet, Lowell, and
the critical brouhaha that Lowell's developing career
provoked. It should be said at once that this pitiably
veering weathercock is not at all the figure that emerges

This article first appeared in the *New York Times Book Review,*
April 25, 1976. © 1975/76 by The New York Times Company.
Reprinted by permission.

from the volume of Berryman's erstwhile uncollected essays and reviews and stories.

For the moment we need take up the matter of Berryman's suicide only so far as to confess ourselves baffled by it—as does Berryman's friend and publisher Robert Giroux, who reveals that a bare seven months before he jumped to his death not only was Berryman assembling this book and getting a new child christened, but he was planning a half-dozen further books to be written through the 1970s. Whatever the reasons for Berryman's suicide, such evidence as we have certainly doesn't *prove* that it was what his writing career was pointing him towards, the only way out that his own poems left open before him. And in fact we look in vain, in Berryman's criticism, for the postures and the arguments or pseudoarguments that are the stock-in-trade of the apologists for a "confessional" or an "extremist" poetry. From 1936, the date of the earliest piece here, through to 1967, the date of the latest, Berryman is thoroughly and unashamedly an *academic* critic and reviewer, though in a way that doesn't preclude his being also a lively and readable journalist. As much could be said of Randall Jarrell, one of Berryman's and Lowell's contemporaries who predeceased them, as did Delmore Schwartz. This was Berryman's generation, and these were his peers—as it seems he was happy to acknowledge.

And after all, to call him "academic" isn't quite good enough. Particularly when he writes of Jewish authors (Anne Frank, Isaac Babel), but in fact throughout, early and late, Berryman is in love with erudition—ultimately with wisdom, but he takes it for granted that the way to wisdom is through erudition; and that erudition is arrived at and transmitted in contexts that are *authoritarian* and *institutional*. Berryman makes this point, as it may be defiantly, by printing in the forefront of this collection and occupying its first eighty pages, the most scholarly articles of all—on Shakespeare and some of his contemporaries; and I think this is a pity. However that may be, Berryman comes through as every inch a university man; there is nothing of the Bohemian about him—it comes naturally to him, writing to a friend in the last year of his life, to give the syllabus of the seminar he is conducting. And it's no surprise to find that a story of his, discovered in his papers, concerns a professor in his classroom teaching Milton's "Lycidas." It's very important, I think, to recognize that none of this testifies to any timidity on Berryman's part, still less to his having in any sense divided aims. For him the vocations of poet and scholar fit together perfectly; and he's in no danger of thinking that the experience he gets from books is less authentic than what he gets from bed or barroom.

On the contrary, a subsidiary but very notable value that this book has, as in effect a chronicle of American literary opinion, is that it should renew our respect for a chapter of American cultural history that at present tends to get condemned as "the New Criticism," if not as "ivory-tower academicism." I have in mind, particularly in essays on Henry James and Theodore Dreiser, Berryman's sharp but respectful dealings with that distinguished suicide of an earlier generation, F. O. Matthiessen. And more important than that, because even more honorable to Berryman, is an exacting implication to that very word *chronicle*, an implication that has everything to do with Berryman's scholarly conscience, his erudition: people have said or done things, books or stories or poems have been written, which deserve to be remembered though they're in danger of being forgotten—and the chronicler recognizes and acts upon the obligation to save them from oblivion. In all of this Berryman's idea of the life devoted to art and to erudition is uncompromisingly austere and strenuous. As he wrote of Ring Lardner in 1956: "All the artists who have ever survived were intellectuals—sometimes intellectuals *also*, but intellectuals. The popular boys cannot understand this. When Shakespeare mocked Chapman and Ralegh and their school of intellectual art, he did it with a higher brow than theirs. Hemingway studied Turgenev and everyone else he thought useful. Lardner never studied anybody." And that is, for Berryman, a death sentence on Lardner.

It's against this severe and inflexible background that we have to make sense of the very fierce and shocking and disconcerting poet that Berryman ultimately became. It cannot be denied that at some point in mid-career Berryman momentously shifted his stance towards his art and the experience that his art fed upon, just as Lowell did with his *Life Studies* (1959). And the shift seems to have to do, not surprisingly, with that inescapable figure in every American poet's heritage, Walt Whitman. Berryman's 1957 essay on Whitman, here printed for the first time and deliberately placed by him so as to introduce all his pieces on modern poetry, is thus a document of capital importance. On the other hand, if Berryman thus belatedly weds himself to the Whitmanesque strain in the American tradition, this doesn't in the least mean—as it too frequently does in what passes for informed discussion on these matters—a rejection of the European, or of "formalism." Berryman remained a poet to whom it came naturally, as late as 1965, to talk of "problems of decorum," and as late as 1968 to go for a title—*His Toy, His Dream, His Rest*—to Giles Farnaby in the sixteenth-century *Fitzwilliam Virginal Book*.

The view of poetry that Berryman reads out of Whitman's *Song of Myself* is what plenty of others have found there: "The poet . . . fills with experience, a valve opens; he speaks them." To the layman this may seem banal, self-evident, and innocuous; it is none of these things, least of all the last—as Berryman undoubtedly recognized when he said, "I am obliged to remark that I prefer this theory of poetry to those that have ruled the critical quarterlies since I was an undergraduate twenty-five years ago." How questionable the Whitman theory is appears when Berryman remarks of it, "It is as humble as, and identical with, Keats's view of the poet as having no existence, but being 'forever in, for, and filling' other things." For only eight years before, in a very perceptive essay on Pound that deserves to be a landmark but isn't, Berryman had cited the same tag from Keats's letters, and had declared austerely: "For poetry of a certain mode (the dramatic), this is a piercing notion; for most other poetry, including Pound's, it is somewhat paradoxical, and may disfigure more than it enlightens." Properly to explain the shift in Berryman between the Pound essay (1949) and the Whitman essay (1957) would go far beyond what can be expected of a reviewer. Let it suffice to say that Berryman isn't muddled, but he's certainly using "dramatic" in a very special sense, since Pound, the creator of "personae," can be seen, and has been, as very much a "dramatic" poet. And in Berryman, the author of *Homage to Mistress Bradstreet* (1956)— which is very clearly in one obvious sense a dramatic, not to say histrionic, performance (and one that as late as 1965 he was deservedly proud of)—the term "dramatic" is obviously a very tricky one. My own guess is that the significance of *Song of Myself* for the later Berryman isn't to be charted in terms of poetic theory, however generously interpreted, but has to do with two aspects of the Whitmanesque poet that have often been remarked on—first, his egalitarianism (his "democracy"), and second, his shamelessness. In that case, the pathos and the distinction of Berryman's career reside first in his having a haughtiness which Whitmanesque democracy was permitted to chastise (in 1947, in Cambridge, England, the lordly urbanity of Berryman of Clare Hall was vividly remembered); and second, in his having a natural shamefastness which Whitmanesque openness was permitted, with the help of alcohol, to outrage.

As a young American in England, nearly forty years ago, Berryman appears to have hopped aboard the Dylan Thomas bandwagon, then vociferously rolling. And it is tempting to date from that experience, not from the encounter with Whitman fifteen years later, Berryman's conversion to some vulgarly debased notion of the poet as society's sacrificial scapegoat. Biographical documentation, yet to come, may establish that indeed the Dylanesque life-style did have its attractions for Berryman. But in the present state of our knowledge it is prudent, as well as charitable, to suppose that the young American—knowledgeable though he undoubtedly was—was bamboozled by the cherished and sedulously promoted fictions of a foreign culture into thinking, for instance, that Dylan represented a Celtic, an indigenously Welsh, imaginative tradition challenging the received and authenticated English establishment. Berryman's 1940 puff of Thomas gives us no evidence one way or the other; it is strangely statistical—"Colours are frequent, especially green, which occurs twenty-eight times and connotes origin, innocence . . . ." The chief interest of this as of some other pieces of the 1940s is to transport those of us who are old enough to remember back to a world in which Lowell's *Lord Weary's Castle* was contemporaneous with *The Selected Writings of Dylan Thomas* (preface by John L. Sweeney, 1947). And indeed:

> Gospel me to the Garden, let me come
> Where Mary twists the warlock with her flowers . . .

This is early Lowell; but might it not be Thomas?

Another piece now printed for the first time, dating from about 1960, is an essay on *Don Quixote*, which I suspect is even more important than the Whitman essay for getting our bearings on the late Berryman. It is extremely scholarly; the learning, though it is worn lightly and deployed only to be serviceable, is very impressive. It is also a profoundly Christian piece of writing, which insists, if I read it right (for it's written with admirable clarity, yet needs to be much pondered), that Cervantes's comic masterpiece comes into focus only if we read it as a work of fervent though disenchanted piety. This is important, because the notion is abroad that Berryman in his last two collections wobbled or wavered into an unconsidered sort of Christian salvationism. On the contrary, his Christian allegiance dates from much farther back in his life. And remembering how the astonishingly sustained six-line stanzas of *The Dream Songs* (1969) make up a minstrel-show colloquy between "Henry" and "Mr. Bones," how can we fail to make the connection with Quixote and his interlocutor Sancho Panza? Berryman's suicide was "quixotic"; just so—and we owe it to him to learn what he thought the quixotic figure signified. (One thing it signified was "humility," as one thing the Whitmanesque figure signified was "humiliation"; and one way to regard all Berryman's poems of the 1960s is as one long penitential exercise in self-humiliation.)

As for death wishes—yes, they do crop up, quite insistently; notably in "Thursday Out," which is presented as a story but seems to be rather a section of travelogue, a highly wrought meditation on that grandest of mausoleums, the Taj Mahal; and in "Shakespeare's Last Word," here printed for the first time, an essay on *The Tempest*. But death wish sounds too glib, too clinically dismissive.

If that is anywhere near the right diagnosis of Berryman's trouble, we can be sure he arrived at it himself long before we did. In any case the possibility doesn't in the least qualify my sense that the man behind this book was not only one of the most gifted and intelligent Americans of his time, but also one of the most honorable and responsible. I take no satisfaction in saying this. The time to say it to him was when he was alive. And now it's too late.

Lowell's *Selected Poems*

"For three decades," says his publisher justly, "Robert Lowell has been regarded as the premier American poet, perhaps the greatest in the English language." This being so, it is almost impossible at this stage not to be mutinous and carping—not to ask oneself, for instance, why it is unthinkable that her Australian publisher should make any such claim for Judith Wright, though she is surely one of Lowell's competitors. Is it not the fact of the American imperium, which Lowell's poems from time to time have castigated so harshly, that makes such a claim plausible, where in the case of the Australian it wouldn't be? Art may or may not be independent of power politics; the making of artists' reputations certainly isn't.

To Dietrich Bonhoeffer at the end of 1942, awaiting imprisonment by the Nazis, it seemed that "unless we have the courage to fight for a revival of wholesome reserve between man and man, we shall perish in an anarchy of human values. The impudent contempt for such reserve is the mark of the rabble. . . ." Lowell's career has run directly contrary to that; he seems to have decided that, however it may be for other people, reserve is what

This article first appeared in the *New York Times Book Review*, July 18, 1976. © 1975/76 by The New York Times Company. Reprinted by permission.

a poet can't afford and must dispense with. In one way Bonhoeffer's option just wasn't open to Lowell. Bearing the name he did, and with such illustrious ancestry behind him, he could never have been altogether a private citizen. And Lowell throughout, from his protest against World War II through to his protest against the Vietnam War, has supposed that his background compelled him into the public arena. He has great family pride, and has lent the luster of his name to public demonstrations on matters of conscience. It is paradoxical, and yet it makes sense, that precisely because he's a patrician, and conscious of it, Lowell has adopted the attitude that Bonhoeffer thought "the mark of the rabble." For Lowell's self-exposure has gone far beyond taking up bold stands on matters of public concern. He has never supposed that a poet was just a leader of opinion; it has always seemed to him that when a poet "takes a stand," he is obliged to convey the whole context of experience which impelled him to do so, including murkily impure motives and obscure compulsions behind even the bravest actions. And this he took to mean that, being born a Lowell, he had lost the right to that private life which more private citizens had the right to, and could safeguard. Accordingly this poet's private life has been lived in public—all the more conspicuously in these last years since his withdrawal to England, when his poetry has turned more and more to domestic and family concerns. One may think that Lowell has read his situation wrongly, and that Bonhoeffer's injunction should have carried weight with him; and one may revere some of his contemporaries and near contemporaries—particularly the great Russians Pasternak and Mandelstam—for having acted so as to strengthen what Bonhoeffer extolled as "reserve." Nevertheless, we can understand and respect the logic that has led Lowell along such a different path.

One reason why the high claims made for Lowell have

been seldom challenged is that he is himself the most modest and magnanimous of men; the generosity of his tributes to his masters, his peers, his juniors is not merely good breeding, still less prudent diplomacy, but is heart-felt—as we see from many touching and splendid poems. Others may make vaunting claims on his behalf; he doesn't make them himself. (He doesn't need to, of course.) In any case, whether or not he is a *preeminently* good writer, he is certainly a very good one—"the distance plighting a tree-lip of land to the islands" is a lovely line; and if "lovely" isn't a word that one often hears from Lowell's admirers, that tells us something about them, not about him. He is consistently more humble, because more traditional, than they are. He will probably concur, for instance, if we make a classroom distinction between texture and structure, and say that the first has never given him much trouble whereas the second always has. Lowell respects classroom distinctions, having spent much time in classrooms. And the fascination of his *Selected Poems*, by any reckoning a momentous book, isn't in seeing classic status finally sealed and settled, but in seeing this poet struggle more strenuously than ever before, and more successfully, with the problem of *structure*.

It has been with him from the first—certainly ever since that gingerbread-Gothic monstrosity, "The Mills of the Kavanaghs," which is here represented by just five sections out of what were originally thirty-eight. But the problem has been particularly pressing in the last decade, when the very title, *Notebook*, advertised Lowell's inability to make out of his recent years of writing any significant shapes, any *structures*, beyond arbitrary cookie-cutter units, each fourteen lines long. In 1973 he worked over this material and hacked out of it two books, *History* and *For Lizzie and Harriet*, neither of them a satisfying structure, still the same journal jottings, though sorted now into two piles. Not everyone objected. For those were the years when one heard a lot about poetry as process, not as product; and about how poetry as process, as infinitely extensible Songs of Myself, was the distinctively American thing. Charles Olson's *Maximus Poems*, Pound's *Cantos*—structureless structures, poems that went on forever until the poet's death put a term to them, poems that never closed but merely *left off*, open-ended—these, it was said, were the characteristic products of the American imagination. And so Lowell's *Notebook*, his *History* and *For Lizzie and Harriet*, could be welcomed as showing that at last he too had emancipated himself from the Europeanized classroom notions that he'd started with, and had become a Whitmanesque all-American boy. But Lowell, it is clear, wasn't persuaded or satisfied. Play around as we may with notions of "the organic," for him a structureless structure remained a contradiction in terms. And I'm delighted to report that, making this *Selected*, he has applied himself again to his unmanageably voluminous and various notebooks, and has at last triumphantly found there at least one structure that is entirely satisfying; twenty-five poems under the title, "Nineteen Thirties," corresponding roughly to pages 104 to 117 of *History*. This is a true sequence, with beginning, middle, and end, with a clearly discernible plot, and above all with a deeply satisfying and plangent *closure*, in the three-line poem, "To Daddy," and the lovely "Will Not Come Back." This is very important—not just as a development in the poet, but because it provides us with a poem of great beauty and great humaneness. For that is the point—"Nineteen Thirties" is one poem in twenty-five parts, a *true* sequence, an achieved structure. And the overall structure, thus extricated, orders every one of its component parts, so that, for instance, "Returning" (*History*, page 115) can now be seen for the first time as the very tightly organized and painfully perceptive statement that it is.

One can also see, throughout this poem and triumphantly at its close, a significant and surely deliberate change in Lowell's metrics—a loosening of the iambic measure not into unmetered sprawl but into wavering trisyllabic cadences, anapestic or dactylic, which Lowell is known to associate particularly with Thomas Hardy. And the opening lines of "Will Not Come Back" recall, in imagery and cadence alike, Hardy's "Afterwards." Hardy, of course, is above all the poet of structures— sometimes quite excessively and constrictingly so, when his structures are overt, in fiercely symmetrical rhyming stanzas. As long ago as *For the Union Dead* Lowell showed himself able to master such structures, in "The Flaw," here very rightly reprinted. This is, however, solidly iambic; and the inwardness of Hardy's structures at their most memorable and compelling is to be registered, not in rhyme schemes but in meter. These inwardly Hardyesque structures are approximated in parts of *History*, where the overt presence of Hardy isn't perceptible at all. A metrical examination of Lowell is still to seek, despite the dozens of critics who have written about him; it would not be an easy exercise, and it would have to be done by somebody with an American ear, not a British one like mine.

Between *For the Union Dead* and *History* there came the octosyllabic couplets of *Near the Ocean*—the most defiantly and conspicuously "traditional" of all the measures that Lowell has used, and elegantly formalized by him into tidy stanzas. Even so, this is necessarily a discursive form, one that doesn't lend itself to intensities; and, because intensity is what Lowell is most admired for, this collection tends to be overlooked. It is the book of his that has always given me most pleasure, which I most envy him. Accordingly I wince at the drastic surgery Lowell has performed on these poems. The most extreme case is "Night in Maine," five stanzas only preserved from the seventeen that it had when it was called "Fourth of July in Maine." Some of the stanzas now omitted were very fine, and in the present version the penultimate stanza seems inadequately prepared for. Similarly, "Central Park," octosyllabic though not in stanzas, has lost twenty-five lines, and in the process lost compassion. Lowell has been too hard on this one of his earlier selves.

It was very much a WASP self, this one, circling—half wistful, half appalled—around New England Protestantism. And the excision of it, of so much of it, removes a counterbalance to the yet earlier, fervently Roman Catholic Lowell who wrote "Colloquy in Black Rock." This reads as well as ever it did—that's to say, very well indeed. It had to be included. And yet its inclusion, and the inclusion of others like it, surely raises questions that are troubling and unanswerable. Auden, when he ceased to believe things he had said in his youth, removed or reversed the lines in which he'd said them. That didn't seem right either. But if one thinks that the issue of Christian belief is a real one (and one needn't be a believer to think so), how does one read a poem which asserts certain matters to be certain and true, when one knows that the poet long ago ceased to believe them so himself? This is a simpleminded question, and therefore (as I've admitted) unanswerable. It's the question: how seriously do we take what a poet or a poem *says*? The question arises only with greatly gifted and persuasive and scrupulous poets. It arises with Lowell.

George Steiner on Language

Some months ago there appeared, in the first issue of the *New Review*, a long letter from George Steiner explaining in effect why he could not respond to the editor's invitation to write for that journal. Though it must have seemed to many people that Steiner lost control of his argument at certain points, yet his wounded diatribe about the present state and future prospects of British literary culture must have struck nearly everybody as a document of the first importance, exceptionally brave, penetrating, and vulnerable; just as the printing of it, so damaging as it was and was meant to be, was an act of exceptional courage on the part of the editor, Ian Hamilton. Among Steiner's accusations was this:

> An unmistakable thinness, corner-of-the-mouth sparsity, sour fastidiousness, have developed in the English intellectual literary tone. The age is less one of anxiety than of envy, of hopeful malice. To borrow an image from a French children's story, the thin gray ones, the steely trimmers, hate the round warm ones. They deride the messiness of intense presence, of intense feeling which they call "flamboyance". They come with tight lips and deflation.

This article first appeared in the London *Times Literary Supplement*, 1974. Reprinted by permission of Times Newspapers Limited.

Because any reviewer faced with a book as big as *After Babel* may feel the need to establish his own position, if not his credentials, I may say that I recognize the tone that is defined by Steiner in his first two sentences and that I want quite vehemently to dissociate myself from its "hopeful malice"; but that, on the other hand, in the terms provided by the French children's story, I recognize myself—not perhaps without some fatuous complacency—as one of the "steely trimmers." Whether I can thus eat my cake and have it is, of course, open to question. But I think I owe it to Professor Steiner thus to declare my hand, more particularly since he has lately been as good as his disparaging word, and has removed himself from the British literary scene to Geneva, for reasons which I understand.

I am provoked to think first about earnestness, "being in earnest." If Dr. Johnson was wrong and naive in his famous refusal to consider that Milton in *Lycidas* might have been in earnest (because, Johnson thought, the use of the pastoral convention precluded it), must we suppose that whatever we take as signs of earnestness in either speech or writing are in fact wholly conventional signs, ultimately arbitrary? Surely we must. For we perceive clearly that what are signs of earnestness in one language are signs of flippancy in another. The difference between British and American English is striking in this respect, and from this and many other points of view British and American must be considered as distinct tongues, though it is not to George Steiner's purpose so to consider them. However that may be, the difficulty that some British readers have had in "taking Steiner seriously"—a difficulty which he is aware of and resents, which he is still trying to remove by trying a new "register," a new style—surely derives, though I'm not sure he realizes it, from his trilingualism, a condition which he presents to us in this book as being, to all intents and purposes, innate. Though we can accept without demur his contention that he is lexically, grammatically, and in deeper ways, too, a native speaker of each of his three languages—French, German, English—I think a consideration of his career as a writer (also, I would guess, as a public speaker) would show that *rhetorically* one of his languages, British English, is *not* native to him. But of course, once we move into the rhetorical dimension of language, we know no longer whether we are speaking of a style of speech or a style of thought; and so some people might want to say that Steiner, though he speaks and writes an English without gallicisms, nonetheless *thinks* like a Frenchman—for "earnest" is a word that can go with "thought" no less than with "feeling" or "speech."

In one language community at some one time, a terse pithiness, a dry or casual tone, and a conversational or colloquial vocabulary are taken for signs that a writer is in earnest; in a neighboring language community, or in the first language at another period, earnestness is signaled on the contrary by copiousness, by "hammering home" (i.e., saying one thing in different ways, many times over), by an excited or urgent tone, and by a vocabulary that darts or ranges all the way from the racy to the ornate and the proudly erudite. Insofar as the accepted signs of earnestness in current English are pithiness, dryness, casualness (and in fact there are probably English-speaking circles where these signs are *not* accepted, and perhaps never have been), George Steiner is still in this book using a foreign rhetoric, one that the steely trimmers among us have been conditioned to distrust. True, Steiner has dried out of his style the effects of restless and lurid chiaroscuro which characterized earlier books like *Language and Silence* and *In Bluebeard's Castle*; and to my English-conditioned taste this is sheer gain. But he is still an eloquent, ornate and *driving* writer, above all a copious one. It is important that as English readers we overcome our conditioned prejudice against such copiousness; overcome, for instance, our feeling that Steiner's book as a whole, and each of its six massive chapters, could and should have been shorter. For we must suppose Steiner, in this book, to be entirely in earnest. We must do this for our own good, not in charity to him—simply because he is saying things we cannot afford not to take note of, and in doing so he is challenging reputations so formidably influential among us as Noam Chomsky's and J. L. Austin's. Moreover, these reputations were made and are maintained in fields quite other than the field, comparative literature, in which Steiner might feel himself professionally "safe"; and so this too we must salute as a sign of earnestness—Steiner has been either brave or rash, he has been at all events *bold*.

Because his style is copious, this author is at one and the same time seductively quotable, and yet not easily quotable *to some purpose*. After tearing my hair a good deal, I excerpt the following passages to represent what I register as his central and most salutary contention. He is speaking of the ancient Greeks, and their view of the relation between truth and language:

One need only recall the enchanted exchanges between Athene and Odysseus in the *Odyssey* (XIII) to realise that mutual deception, the swift saying of "things which are not" need be neither evil nor a bare tactical constraint. Gods and chosen mortals can be virtuosos of mendacity, contrivers of elaborate untruths for the sake of the verbal craft (a key, slippery term) and intellectual energy involved. The classical world was only too ready to document the fact that the Greeks took an aesthetic or sporting view of lying. A very ancient conception of the vitality of "mis-statement" and "mis-understanding," of the primordial affinities between language and dubious meaning, seems implicit in the notorious style of Greek oracles. . . .

In short, a seminal, profound intuition of the creativity of falsehood, an awareness of the organic intimacy between the genius of speech and that of fiction, of "saying the thing which is not", can be traced in various aspects of Greek mythology, ethics, and poetics. . . . But from Stoicism and early Christianity onward, "feigning", whose etymology is so deeply grounded in "shaping" (*fingere*), has been in very bad odour.

This may account for the overwhelming one-sidedness of the logic and linguistics of sentences. To put it in a crude, obviously figurative way, the great mass of common speech-events . . . do not fall under the rubric of "factuality" and truth. The very concept of integral truth—"the whole truth and nothing but the truth"—is a fictive ideal of the courtroom or the seminar in logic. Statistically, the incidence of "true statements"—definitional, demonstrative, tautological—in any given mass of discourse is probably small. The current of language is intentional, it is instinct with purpose in regard to audience and situation. It aims at attitude and assent. . . . We communicate motivated images, local frameworks of feeling. . . . We speak less than the truth, we fragment in order to reconstruct desired alternatives, we select and elide. It is not "the things which are" that we say, but those which might be, which we would bring about, which the eye and remembrance compose. . . . Information does not come naked except in the schemata of computer languages or the lexicon. It comes attenuated, flexed, coloured, alloyed by intent and the milieu in which the utterance occurs (and "milieu" is here the total biological, cultural, historical, semantic ambience as it conditions the moment of individual articulation).

We may pause here for a reflection that will seem spiteful, but is not. To put it demurely, the conveying of accurate information has never been one of the things for which we have valued Steiner's writings; and before I am through I shall have to notice an instance of misinformation in this very book. But the conveying of information is not—so Steiner powerfully argues—anything but a marginal and highly specialized function of language. And so the passage just quoted can be seen as exculpation, self-justification, very adroit and telling.

The direction of Steiner's argument is in any case very clear:

> In brief: I am suggesting that the outwardly communicative, extrovert thrust of language is secondary and that it may in substantial measure have been a later socio-historical acquirement. The primary drive is inward and domestic.
>
> Each tongue hoards the resources of consciousness, the world-pictures of the clan. Using a simile still deeply entrenched in the language-awareness of Chinese, a language builds a wall around the "middle kingdom" of the group's identity. It is secret towards the outsider and inventive of its own world. Each language selects, combines and "contradicts" certain elements from the total potential of perceptual data. This selection, in turn, perpetuates the differences in world images explored by Whorf. . . . There have been so many thousands of human tongues, there still are, because there have been, particularly in the archaic stages of social history, so many distinct groups intent on keeping from one another the inherited, singular springs of their identity, and engaged in creating their own semantic worlds. . . .
>
> Most probably there is a common molecular biology and neuro-physiology to all human utterance. It seems very likely that all languages are subject to constraints and similarities determined by the design of the brain, by the vocal equipment of the species and, it might be, by certain highly generalized, wholly abstract efficacies of logic, of optimal form, and relation. But the ripened humanity of language, its indispensable conservative and creative force lie in the extraordinary diversity of actual tongues, in the bewildering profusion and eccentricity (though there is no centre) of their modes. The psychic need for particularity, for "in-clusion" and in-

vention is so intense that it has, during the whole of man's history until very lately, outweighed the spectacular, obvious material advantages of mutual comprehension and linguistic unity. . . .

It follows . . . that the poem, taking the word in its fullest sense, is neither a contingent nor a marginal phenomenon of language. A poem concentrates, it deploys with least regard to routine or conventional transparency, those energies of covertness and of invention which are the crux of human speech.

With that last resounding contention, it comes clear how the whole ambitious arc of Steiner's argument—it has taken him over two hundred pages to get to this point—should have arisen out of his professional field of comparative literature to which, at this point, it returns. And it may be thought that we have heard this before, from other scholars and teachers with a vested interest in the study of literature, rather than linguistics or philosophy, communications theory or semiotics or computer science or three or four other disciplines which nowadays set their sights all or some of the time on the phenomenon of human language. But in fact there is a notable difference between this sentiment as we hear it from Steiner and as we have heard it from others. For in the first place those two hundred pages have not been wasted, but have been spent by this literary scholar in reviewing those other studies, one after another, so as to substantiate his charge that all are characterized by "overwhelming one-sidedness." In the second place he has insisted that the condition of the polyglot is—not statistically, of course, but logically—more normal than the monoglot condition, for any responsible study of language. And the truth is (though this is my point, not Steiner's) that this is no more of a challenge and a reproach to current habits in linguistics and linguistic philosophy, than it is to much or most study of language under the auspices of literature—where indeed a sort of linguistic chauvinism has lately become not just common practice but, in some energetic circles, positively a required duty.

Moreover, the central perception—that the function of human languages is, quite properly and necessarily, more to conceal than to reveal—reaches out into quite other areas. Hannah Arendt, for example, discussing in *Of Violence* what changes *engagés* into *enragés*, decides, "it is not injustice that ranks first, but hypocrisy. . . ." And, maintaining that a resort to violence from these motives is "not irrational," she declares, "words can be relied on only if one is sure that their function is to reveal and not to conceal." But Steiner contends, and so far as I am concerned he proves, that the assurance which Hannah Arendt here asks for on behalf of the *enragés* is one that can never be given. For their "hypocrisy" we should read "duplicity," and a duplicity which is of the nature of human language as such, since nothing else explains the multiplicity of tongues that humankind does speak. Thus the *enragés* are asking for the impossible. But, in the first place, they could have been brought to ask for it by listening to linguisticians and philosophers, even (I'm afraid) to literary critics; and second, they would, if they were sincere and intelligent, be less likely to ask for this impossibility if they knew something other than a monoglot culture. (Moreover, in an extended but justifiable sense, our culture is becoming more completely monoglot with each year that passes. The legitimizing of the four-letter words in the name of the sexual revolution—their newly public currency hailed as enlightenment—plainly represents a deliberately covert language made overt and public.)

As regards poetry, while Steiner's argument obviously

and powerfully validates poetry that is hermetic and arcane, it does not elevate it over a poetry that aspires to be limpid and readily accessible, even readily translatable. (Steiner establishes—indeed, it is the first point he makes, and abundantly demonstrates—that to gain *access* to calculated utterances in one's native tongue itself involves, very crucially, acts of translation.) If language of its nature covers up as much as it opens out, the poet who aspires to be lucid will find necessarily, in his medium, enough to frustrate that aspiration—as many a poet can mournfully testify, having seen what he took to be as plain as a pikestaff converted, by reasonably attentive readers, into something as gnarled and convoluted as a yew tree. Steiner doubtless would agree to this, and yet his heart might not be in it. For he is, as he always was, excited by extreme situations in art and by the extremists who provoke and contrive them. Thus we do not have to wait long, after he has descended to particular cases of interlingual translators and translations, before we find him saying: "But Hölderlin pressed further. He was trying to move upstream not only to the historical springs of German but to the primal energies of human discourse." Though his examination of Hölderlin as translator and Broch as self-translator establishes quite fairly his challenging and crucial contention that "literalism is not, as in traditional models of translation, the naive, facile mode but, on the contrary, the ultimate," nevertheless some readers may detect a foreign style of feeling, too much of "the messiness of intense presence," in the evident excitement with which Steiner approaches all cases of "pressing further."

This foreignness might be defined by saying that Steiner is rather seldom concerned that translation be *serviceable*. And yet, to this too there are exceptions. It is just hereabouts, in his chapter five, that he provides several scintillating yet wholly self-explanatory pages

which could and should be put in the hands of any trans-
lator, from the merest beginner to the most profession-
ally accomplished, pages concerned simply with French,
German, and English at the level of the tourist's phrase
book, demonstrating how it is impossible to translate "I
like swimming" or "it looks like rain" or "the child has
been run over" without "falsification"—that is to say,
without running one's head at once into the inherent
biases not just of French language, German language but
of French *culture*, German *culture*. The touching thing
here—though in fact the poignancy informs the whole
book—is that Steiner, whose trilingualism shows him
how "impossible" translation is, nevertheless affirms
that it must be possible because it is necessary, with a
necessity that is inherent in the human condition.

He says that *After Babel* originated in the *Penguin
Book of Modern Verse Translation*, which he edited in
1966. If we look back at his introduction to that anthol-
ogy, we see that on certain crucial issues he has changed
his mind. This is high praise, of a sort that one cannot
often give—least of all to a writer who conceives of him-
self as embattled, as Steiner plainly does. To look again,
to think again, to allow that certain objections are just—
this is particularly difficult and honorable in someone
who feels himself isolated, and under attack. Thus, in
After Babel, we are no longer told that "the period from
Rossetti to Robert Lowell has been an age of poetic trans-
lation rivalling that of the Tudor and Elizabethan mas-
ters"; and in fact we now come across references to
Lowell that are sharply disparaging, as well as many that
are admiring. More momentously, Steiner has abandoned
the working definition of 1966, when he declared (his
italics):

> I have taken translation to include *the writing of a poem in
> which a poem in another language (or in an earlier form of*

> *one's own language) is the vitalizing, shaping presence; a poem which can be read and responded to independently but which is not ontologically complete, a previous poem being its occasion, begetter, and in the literal sense raison d'etre.*

The trouble with such a definition is not that it is demonstrably wrong (for of course it isn't), but that it is *useless*; it comprehends too much, excludes too little, for it to be a serviceable tool in any circumstances one can conceive of. And what is the point of a working definition that can never be set to work? In *After Babel* Steiner has retreated to the commonsense position that (however many borderline cases crop up, as of course they do) there is translation properly or strictly considered, and on the other hand—across a frontier which exists, though we cannot always find it—all those other traffickings between poems which we gesture at in words like "running allusion," "imitation," "adaptation," "parody," "pastiche," "burlesque," "variation." Of course there's no need for him to give up his fervent interest in these transactions. He devotes his last chapter to them, arguing eloquently and movingly that the progeny through the centuries of forms and themes first defined for the most part in ancient Greece (he traces some of the lines of descent) constitutes a continuity and integrity in western Europe from at least the fifth century B.C. to at least the twentieth A.D. (About the twenty-first he has alarming apprehensions, which it is hard not to share.) Though to a student of literature this phase of his argument is less novel and arresting than earlier stages, here too is much that is instructive and provocative—notably a brief but exhilarating treatment of musical settings for poems as being in some sense (and who can deny it?) *translations* of those poems. Nor should anyone want to deny Steiner his conviction that all these transactions—imitations, parodies, "settings"—are kinds of translation, in the sense that the areas they denote are what we get into as soon as we cross the frontier from translation proper. We might even concede that the distinction between "translation" and "imitation" is a distinction merely of convenience. But "convenience" matters—*our* convenience, as readers and thinkers, as translators and poets. This is what one means by asking that any discussion of these baffling matters be *serviceable*; and the discussion in *After Babel* is serviceable, as the discussion in the Penguin anthology wasn't, and couldn't be.

It should be clear by now that I greatly admire the intellectual venture which this book represents—so boldly sustained, so vulnerably extended; that I esteem it as of quite another order from Steiner's earlier writings, or from such as I have read. That said, I must point out how difficult he makes it for his admirers. Probably he has been at more pains to protect himself in the many areas he invades where I cannot check on him, than in the area of concerns which, as it happens, we share. But it is on page fifteen—as early as that, in a book of nearly five hundred pages—that I find him writing as follows, of our alleged inability nowadays to respond fairly to D. G. Rossetti, Swinburne, Lionel Johnson, and others of their generations:

> Much more is involved here than a change of fashion, than the acceptance by journalism and the academy of a canon of English poetry chosen by Pound and Eliot. This canon is already being challenged; the primacy of Donne may be over, Browning and Tennyson are visibly in the ascendant. A design of literature which finds little worth commending between Dryden and Hopkins is obviously myopic.

Here, though I hate to say it, just about everything is wrong that could be. In the first place, neither Eliot nor Pound *did* choose or establish "a canon." It is not, one might say, an activity that poets are prone to. Whatever phantasmal canon may be thought to be currently established among us, or to have been so established until lately, was defined and disseminated not by Pound nor by Eliot, but by their mostly academic epigones, who have systematized and made categorical certain animadversions and preferences thrown out by the two poets in passing, or at any rate in the context of highly specific occasions. Secondly, insofar as there has come into being by this process a Poundian and an Eliotic "canon," they diverge radically: whereas an Eliotic canon would indeed exclude Swinburne, Rossetti, and Lionel Johnson, a Poundian canon would in fact find an honorable place (though not equally honorable) for each of these poets and for the poetic idiom which each of them stands for. Thirdly, the astrological metaphor—"Browning and Tennyson are visibly in the ascendant"—should not obscure the fact that what Steiner is talking about is precisely what he denies, "a change of fashion." To be specific, the novel interest and pleasure that some of us can now take, thanks to Christopher Ricks, in certain poems of Tennyson rests immediately on our no longer having to repudiate the idea that Tennyson is of the company of Virgil and Milton; we see and can relish what a past poet has to offer, only when inflated claims for him have been exploded. As for "the primacy of Donne" and "a design of literature which finds little worth commending between Dryden and Hopkins," surely these chimeras never existed outside the heated imagination of George Steiner. Barbarianized as we are, surely no one even remotely reputable ever claimed for Donne "primacy" over Shakespeare or Chaucer? And who ever found "little worth commending" be-

tween Dryden and Hopkins? How much is "little"?
Is Wordsworth "little"? How much of Wordsworth is
"little"? One has only to phrase these questions to see
that we are moving in a world of what is *à la mode*, not
at all in a world of responsible intellectual endeavor.

The truth is that George Steiner, now as in the past,
can veer disconcertingly from genuine intellectual eleva-
tion and rigor to what one can only call *vulgarity*. Some-
where in his head there is the image of a mittel-European
or else mid-Atlantic bourse, where every living writer, as
well as many dead ones, is quoted at a certain selling
price; and for these "quotations" Steiner has an unac-
countable respect. His word for them, sometimes, is
"canonical." Pound's *Cantos*, it seems, are still going dirt-
cheap (a "laboured, ultimately sterile exercise"); on the
other hand, Pound's *Homage to Sextus Propertius* still
commands a high price—though as a translation, which
it surely isn't, but rather a quite deliberate, highly inven-
tive, and instructive *travesty*. In any case it is this stock-
exchange fantasy which accounts, in *After Babel*, for
such bizarre parentheses as "Paul Celan, almost certainly
the major European poet of the period after 1945"; or,
"the modal completeness of French literature (major per-
formances in every genre)." It explains too, in Steiner's
letter to the *New Review*, the lordly interjection, "No
one since D. H. Lawrence being at once 'English English'
and, beyond cavil, of world rank,"—a ticker-tape readoff
which reappears, in *After Babel*, as a rhetorical question:
"Has there been an 'English English' author of absolutely
the first rank after D. H. Lawrence and J. C. Powys?"
What is sad about this last instance is that Steiner, when
handing down this judgment, is in no sense swimming
against the tide but, on the contrary, as he must realize,
is the spokesman of an inert consensus. For thirty years
at least the English have been telling themselves that
they neither have, nor can expect to have, writers of the

status of D. H. Lawrence—precarious as *that* status is, in all conscience. And by now that proposition, parroted unthinkingly through several generations, has most of the characteristics of a self-fulfilling prophecy. What is even more mournfully comical is that this predetermined view of "English English" writing, voluntarily subscribed to by Steiner, appears to originate in just that "corner-of-the-mouth sparsity, sour fastidiousness" which he declares himself at odds with, and unable to stomach. For my part, insofar as I can give any substance to the notion of "world rank" or "first rank," I do so by recalling opinions that I have heard expressed by non-British people who have shown themselves to be both informed and exacting readers of English; and on that basis I report—for what it is worth, which is little—that four or five of my "English English" contemporaries, some writing verse, some prose, seem to be generally accorded the rank that Steiner would deny them.

All of this is a pity, but in the last analysis it isn't important. George Lukacs, writing *The Historical Novel*, muddles one Walter Scott novel with another, and is only intermittently and imperfectly aware that the history of Scotland and the history of England differ. And what could be more vulgar, in the bleakest sense, than for Lukacs in the 1950s to have lent his investigations of literary genre and literary history to the specious purposes of a "common front for peace," under the sinister auspices of Picasso's dove-with-olive-branch? Never mind! Lukacs belongs securely in a tradition of high-flying speculation about literature, which we costive islanders cannot afford not to profit by. In such cases the chain of reasoning is emphatically *not* as strong as its weakest link. George Steiner belongs in that tradition also; and with this eloquent and earnest book he earns a place in it as securely as Lukacs.

Six Notes on Ezra Pound

EZRA AMONG THE EDWARDIANS

If I wanted to be pretentious, I might call this paper an investigation of the sociology of literature. It is at any rate a sketch of what might be involved in restoring a writer—in this case, the young Pound—to the highly specific social milieu, that of Edwardian England, in which he moved and on which he impinged. It is thus a contribution to biography, not to criticism.

Among Pound's associates in that vanished world, the most intructive figures, I'm inclined to think, are Frederic Manning and Allen Upward; but unfortunately we're still very far from recovering from oblivion the lineaments of either of these men. (Recovering them is a matter of great urgency; and a start has been made, but there's a long way to go—especially with Upward, whom oblivion has enveloped with a completeness that is startling and significant.) Since Manning and Upward are in this way for the moment denied us, I shall make do with two other names: Maurice Hewlett and Laurence Binyon. And Hewlett is the one to start with, probably the best

This article first appeared in *Paideuma*, 5, no. 1 (1976).

peg on which to hang a necessarily rash characterization of that literary world of late-Edwardian England which Fred Manning entered from Australia, and Pound from the United States.

Not that Hewlett was a representative figure, if by that we mean a sort of undistinguished average. On the contrary he was taken to be something of a maverick and flutterer of dovecotes. Or so it appears from the valuable memoirs of Mrs. Belloc Lowndes, in chapter nine of her *Merry Wives of Westminster*:

> On the whole he had a poor opinion of human nature, and he felt an angry contempt for politicians. Indeed he was apt to take violent prejudices against certain men and women in public life with whom he was not personally acquainted. On many a winter morning I jumped out of bed and put a letter of his in the fire, feeling it would be wrong to allow it to survive; and when some years ago I was asked by a distinguished man of letters if I could help him to write an account of Maurice Hewlett, I rashly said I would send him some of the letters I had received from him. But when I looked over those I had kept, I decided I could not do so.

If many of Hewlett's correspondents felt as Mrs. Lowndes did, this explains why Hewlett's letters as edited by Laurence Binyon (1925) make such unexciting reading; she herself records that of the three hundred letters printed by Binyon there was only one "which I felt to be characteristic of the man I knew so well." Binyon's volume does however bear out quite touchingly one point that Mrs. Lowndes makes: that Hewlett's ambition was to be known as poet rather than novelist, though it was his historical romances in Wardour Street prose that brought him fame and money. (And some of those romances were set in medieval Aquitaine of the troubadours—which certainly constitutes one common interest that drew Pound and Hewlett together.)

Hewlett and Mrs. Lowndes moved in the same influential circles. And Pound was not above using his connection with Hewlett so as to get entry to those circles. Thus in a letter to his father of 3 June 1913, all the names are of people who figure in Mrs. Lowndes's memoirs:

> We had a terribly literary dinner on Saturday. Tagore, his son and daughter-in-law, Hewlett, May Sinclair, Prothero (edt. *Quarterly Rev.*) Evelyn Underhill (author of divers fat books on mysticism), *D.* and myself.

The name to give us pause here is that of G. W. Prothero. For Prothero is the demon-king of the Poundian pantomime, ever since Pound cast him for this role by printing, at the end of his essay on De Gourmont—originally in the *Little Review*, then in *Instigations* (1920)—the letter which Prothero wrote him in October 1914:

> Dear Mr. Pound,
>   Many thanks for your letter of the other day. I am afraid that I must say frankly that I do not think I can open the columns of the Q.R.—at any rate, at present—to any one associated publicly with such a publication as *Blast*. It stamps a man too disadvantageously.
> Yours truly,
G. W. Prothero
>
> Of course, having accepted your paper on the *Noh*, I could not refrain from publishing it. But other things would be in a different category.

And Pound understandably gets all the mileage possible out of the ill-starred history of "*QR*":

> I need scarcely say that *The Quarterly Review* is one of the most profitable periodicals in England, and one of one's best "connections", or sources of income. It has, of course, a tradition.

"It is not that Mr. Keats (if that be his real name, for we almost doubt that any man in his senses would put his real name to such a rhapsody)"—wrote their Gifford of Keats' *Endymion*. My only comment is that the *Quarterly* has done it again. Their Mr. A. Waugh is a lineal descendant of Gifford, by the way of mentality. A century has not taught them manners. In the eighteen-forties they were still defending the review of Keats. And more recently Waugh has lifted up his senile slobber against Mr. Eliot. It is indeed time that the functions of both English and American literature were taken over by younger and better men.

As for their laying the birch on my pocket, I compute that my support of Lewis and Brzeska has cost me at the lowest estimate about £20 per year, from one source alone since that regrettable occurrence, since I dared to discern a great sculptor and a great painter in the midst of England's artistic desolation. ("European and Asiatic papers please copy.")

Waugh's "senile slobber" against Eliot—he as good as called Eliot "a drunken helot"—has been remarked on several times, notably in his son Evelyn's autobiography, *A Little Learning*.

Prothero the demon-king has never bounded on to the stage more sulphurously than in Hugh Kenner's *The Pound Era*:

Abstract and remote though the contents of *Blast* might be, the establishment had bared its fangs and invoked its ultimate weapon, the boycott. To men who lived on what they could pick up from articles and reviews, the ultimate weapon implied more than lack of a showcase: it implied starvation. . . . Prothero was snarling like a guilty thing surprised. Of what was he guilty? Of reverence for death, or perhaps decorum. . . . The long-term psychic damage Pound underwent is beyond calculation. On the continent men were soon killing each other. A third of a million Frenchmen died in the first five months. . . .

Hugh Kenner doesn't need to be told how much I admire *The Pound Era*. Accordingly I ought to be able to say that at this stage his comments seem to me beside the point, or more exactly in excess of it. What with all this baring of fangs and of ultimate weapons, these snarlings and "long-term psychic damage," how is one to protest mildly that Prothero is—with an engagingly archaic elegance ("stamps a man too disadvantageously")—telling Pound that he needn't waste his time submitting manuscripts to the *Quarterly Review* for the time being? Would it have been more honorable for Prothero to let Pound go on submitting, when there was no hope of his being accepted? It helps, I think, to take note of Conrad Aiken on "Ezra Pound: 1914" (*Ezra Pound: Perspectives*, ed. Stock, 1965):

> But it was typical of Pound's kindness, even to a potential enemy or rival, that he should have so persisted in trying to give me the right contacts.
>
> Contacts: yes, these, as I was to discover, were of prime importance; they were part of the *game*. And for Pound it *was* a game, a super-chess game, and not without its Machiavellian elements. For example, this was the summer of the famous *Blast* dinner for the Vorticists, in which Wyndham Lewis was of course much involved. Pound sent me a card, which I still have, naming place and date, and saying, rather peremptorily, "I think you had better take this in." This put my back up. I had no intention then, or ever after, of joining any group or "movement" and I therefore sidestepped the Vorticists just as I sidestepped both the Imagists and the Amygists. I didn't attend the dinner, for which in a way I'm now sorry, and Pound never forgot or forgave. Nineteen years later, in an angry letter from Italy about some review I'd written which began: "Jesus Gawd Aiken, you poor blithering ass" he concluded by saying: "I've never forgotten that you wouldn't go to the *Blast* dinner."

It was a game, which Pound had played trickily and with zest. When he joined in with *Blast*, he miscalculated and overplayed his hand. And just that, nothing more, is what Prothero is telling him. If the game was for high stakes, if Pound's livelihood was at stake, the more reason for playing the game circumspectly. He didn't; and he paid the price. What is there in this to evoke the shades of a third of a million dead Frenchmen? Or to make a Lucifer figure out of G. W. Prothero?

It could be argued that *Blast* was a miscalculation all round, even for Wyndham Lewis. Certainly it was for Pound. And Violet Hunt, loyally selling copies at half-price in her drawing room, confesses in her memoir *I Have This to Say* that she was at a loss to explain why the damned were damned, and the blest were blest. Among the blest, "Lady Aberconway was put in to please me," and "Madame Strindberg, who ran the Club of the Golden Calf for the sake of the set, could hardly escape a favourable mention. . . . " But "Mrs. Belloc Lowndes felt, I am sure, that she needed no blessings from anyone but her Church." On the other hand, among those blasted, if one understood well enough about "Rabindranath Tagore, from whose recitations ad infinitum we all suffered a great deal about this time," why pick on Thomas Beecham, who at this time with the backing of Lady Cunard was embarking on a lifelong crusade for English opera? Hugh Kenner veers unexpectedly into the idiom of the British schoolboy: "*Blast* should have been a great lark." But even a schoolboy's jape is supposed to have some ascertainable point; and *Blast* had none.

As for Hewlett, how far he knew that he was being "used" by Pound is what at this point no one can determine. I'd guess that he knew, and didn't resent it. For "the game" was one that everyone played, and that was all right so long as you took your losses without squealing. In any case it didn't preclude, on Pound's part, genuine affection. As we see from canto 74:

> Lordly men are to earth o'ergiven
>   these the companions:
> Fordie that wrote of giants
>   and William who dreamed of nobility
>   and Jim the comedian singing:
>   "Blarney castle me darlin'
>   you're nothing now but a stOWne"
> and Plarr talking of mathematics
>   or Jepson lover of jade
> Maurie who wrote historical novels
>   and Newbolt who looked twice bathed
>   are to earth o'ergiven.
>   [432:459]

Later in the *Pisan Cantos* (80/515:550) we read of "that Christmas at Maurie Hewlett's"—Christmas 1911 in Hewlett's fifteenth-century house outside Salisbury—to which Pound was driven from Southampton across a tract of Hardy's Wessex which his imagination peopled with phantoms out of *Under the Greenwood Tree*. Henry Newbolt was at this time Hewlett's neighbor in Wiltshire, and it seems to have been at this Christmas time that Hewlett took Pound to see Newbolt, who figures elsewhere in canto 80:

> "He stood", wrote Mr. Newbolt, later Sir Henry,
> "the door behind" and now they complain of cummings.
>   [507:541]

But the Pisan ordeal had shocked Pound into recovering a compassion and tenderness which we look for mostly in vain in the Pound of the years preceding. And in the 1930s he had been unforgiving towards these friends of his youth. In 1939, for instance, in an obituary of Ford for *The Nineteenth Century and After*, he had written of "the stilted language that then passed for 'good English' in the arthritic milieu that held control of the respected British critical circles, Newbolt, the backwash of Lionel Johnson, Fred Manning, the Quarterlies and the rest of 'em.'" And this echoed a letter of 1937 to Michael Roberts, extolling Ford and saying, "The old crusted lice and advocates of corpse language knew that *The English Review* existed." In *Ezra Pound: The Image and the Real*, Herbert Schneidau reasonably enough names three of the "crusted lice" as Henry Newbolt, Frederic Manning, and G. W. Prothero, and with a proper scrupulousness he notes that all these "were treated with great deference in Pound's early letters and writings."

Schneidau follows Pound's own broad hints by tracing his gradual alienation or liberation from these early admirations according as Ford's demands for a prosaic strength in verse writing gradually won Pound over from the Wardour Street language of his own early poems (such as "Canzone: The Yearly Slain," written in reply to Manning's "Korè"). The story is an intricate one, as Herbert Schneidau acknowledges; and Pound's holding out against Ford for the Dantesque principle of a "curial" diction (see his introduction to the poems of Lionel Johnson) represents to my mind an objection that can still be raised to Ford's principles of diction, salutary as Ford's polemics undoubtedly were for Pound at this time. Moreover Prothero, a historian, perhaps had no ideas about poetic diction one way or the other; Pound, as we have seen, thought himself victimized by Prothero not for anything to do with writing but for having championed Lewis the painter and Gaudier the sculptor. All the same Schneidau's argument is just and illuminating, so far as it goes.

But does it go far enough? It is worth looking again at Pound's letter to Michael Roberts, strident though it is. Pound there, it is plain—for instance, in his comment on Hilaire Belloc—is as unwilling as any Marxist to abstract a question like the proper language for poetry from the whole social matrix and milieu in which such a subject may get itself debated. Pound speaks of the "order of a pewked society." And indeed it is, for us too, evasive and misleading to abstract the manageably limited issue from the larger one. For instance, nothing is more likely than that Prothero, when he said that association with *Blast* "stamped a man too disadvantageously," had in mind among other things Ford's connection with the magazine and the scandal of Ford's relations with Violet Hunt—a scandal that had already made a breach between Violet Hunt and the cruelly timorous Henry James, as told painfully in *I Have This to Say*.

This is where Mrs. Belloc Lowndes is so illuminating. She writes well, though carelessly. And in *The Merry Wives of Westminster*, knowing just what she is doing, she recreates a world as exotic as that of the Andaman Islanders: the world of cultured Edwardian London. I am not concerned to defend that world; I am merely trying to understand it, and the rules by which it lived. Some features of that world are nowadays entirely inscrutable—notably, what it was in Frederic Lowndes's self-effacing position on *The Times* which gave him and his wife access to a society of international aristocracy and even royalty, and to the inner circles of the cabinet, as well as the society of novelists and playwrights. What is clear is that this was all *one* society, in which the wives—like Mrs. Lowndes herself—wrote books or maintained salons, while their husbands were functionaries, some of them much in the public eye as ministers of the Crown, others—like Frederic Lowndes—no less influential and esteemed for operating under wraps, as grey eminences. Barrie and Arnold Bennett, Hewlett and Henry James, were free of this society whenever they chose. It was "the establishment," or one very thick and influential layer of it; but it certainly was not made up of stuffed shirts and Colonel Blimps along with their twittering wives. Indeed, if we can suppress the automatic "liberal" prejudice which indexes "Newbolt, Sir Henry (1862-1938)" as "English imperialist poet" (in *Ezra Pound. Penguin Critical Anthology*, ed. Sullivan), we have to acknowledge that it was in many ways an attractive society, and an admirable one. That we are dealing with a privileged élite goes without saying; as also that it depended on the institution of domestic service. But there appears not to have been, for instance, any of that sterile rivalry between man and wife which is now the bane of middle-class society with any claims to cultural or intellectual interests; plainly Mrs. Lowndes and the young matrons who were her friends did not seethe resentfully at having their intellectual and imaginative capacities shackled to kitchen and nursery, whereas their husbands could exercise theirs in the great world. Moreover—and more to the point—if as literary intellectuals we feel frustrated at having no channel of access to the figures who exercise decision-making power in our societies, Mrs. Lowndes shows us a society in which literary intelligence had direct access to such centers of power, by way of the conjugal bed as well as over the dinner table. Pound—thanks to Hewlett probably more than anyone else—had, at the time of his dinner party for Hewlett and Prothero and the rest, the chance of moving into that society. His espousal of *Blast* closed to him just those doors that were on the point of opening; and twenty years later, when he desperately wanted such access to the power-wielding centers of society, he was condemned to the world of fantasy in which he thought he could influence United States policy by way of such unlikely intermediaries as Senators Borah and Bankhead, and Italian policy by way of Ubaldo degli Uberti.

(This is not to say that Pound's decision was wrong. For Eliot, who chose the other way, earned entry into nothing more seriously influential than the circles of Bloomsbury, where the Edwardian pattern survived only in an attenuated and largely illusory version.)

If we ask what it was about this society which made Pound and also Lewis affront it more or less deliberately, to ensure that its doors were closed to them, I think only one answer is possible: it was ineradicably vowed to the idea of the artist as the amateur. It is true that Arnold Bennett, for one, refused to conform to that stereotype; and doubtless one could find other exceptions. But it is plain that in Mrs. Lowndes's society, writing, for instance, was conceived of as typically a spare-time activity. It could not be otherwise if literary intelligence was to make itself available in drawing rooms to administrative and political decision making. That English tradition of the amateur is of course a long one, and by no means ignoble, reaching back as it does through John Morley to Walter Bagehot, to Burke, to Addison, and so all the way to Philip Sidney and the Renaissance all-round man. But both Pound and Lewis were American or Americanized enough to have on the contrary a *professional* attitude to their respective arts, in the quite precise sense that they saw the continuity of art traditions ensured by the *atelier*, the master instructing his prentices. The renegade or maverick Englishmen with whom they allied themselves—Ford, and at another level A. R. Orage—shared this un-English conviction and habit. And this difference between them and such initially sympathetic Englishmen as Hewlett and Newbolt went very deep; for ultimately it meant that, when the question arose whether the artist's first responsibility was to his art (his *trade*) or to his society, Pound and Lewis and Ford would opt for the first alternative, Hewlett and Newbolt for the second—as indeed we soon see them doing when both of them answer the call of First World War patriotism by writing morale-building poems and stories. It is not hard to see that in *Homage to Sextus Propertius* Pound is centrally concerned with just this question, and is defending his own scale of priorities against Hewlett's or Newbolt's.

Something had certainly gone wrong—gone soft and mawkish—with the English tradition of the amateur, when we find Hewlett on facing pages of Binyon's volume of *Letters*, writing in 1916 to E. V. Lucas, "My Dear Lad, That will be jolly indeed," and to J. C. Squire, "Dear Squire, I am very glad to have your quire of poetry . . . which is in jolly type and on jolly paper. . . ." It is not thus, one cannot help feeling, that the serious artist addresses a fellow practitioner. And even before the War, though Hewlett in correspondence with Harold Monro and Newbolt could give and take hard knocks by way of semitechnical criticism, yet it is enveloped and emasculated by similarly anxious camaraderie. Still, Newbolt at any rate was able to understand something of what was at stake. In his "A Study of English Poetry," which ran in *The English Review* from March to June 1912, Newbolt refers to Pound as "a critic, who is himself a poet, and whom I always read with great interest." Those who think of Pound as a great liberator from stiff and hidebound conventions will be disconcerted to find that Newbolt on the contrary treats him as an academic formalist. Newbolt says:

> The vast majority of what are generally called well-educated persons in this country have, in the very process of their

education, been impressed with the belief that metre is an arrangement of language which can be judged by the application of a mechanical test, and that the poet who produces a line which does not answer to the test is a fit subject for correction by any critic who can point out the discrepancy. It is true that we are more enlightened than we were; there is a public which has learnt to smile at the reviewer who declares that a line "will not scan," or that it contains a "trochee" where it should have had an "iamb," without considering whether it was ever intended to "scan," or whether there is anything in English verse which can be treated as the absolute equivalent of a Greek or Latin trochee. But . . . the fallacy does appear, in much subtler forms. In the *Poetry Review* for February, 1912, a critic, who is himself a poet, and whom I always read with great interest, speaks of the struggle "to find out what has been done, once for all, better than it can ever be done again, and to find out what remains for us to do". . . . But if every work of art is simply the expression of the artist's intuition, it is evident that an absolute or complete pattern would be useless, since the intuitions of two different minds could never be expressed by the same form: nor can anything in art be said to have been "done once for all," since if it were "done again" by another hand—used, that is, to express the intuition of another spirit—it would be no longer what had been done before.

Newbolt's attitude is still very common—not only among the British (especially those who have come under the influence of F. R. Leavis), but also among American free versifiers who think they are an avant-garde and who are muddled enough to think that they have Pound's authority to back them. Whether they know it or not, they are in fact endorsing Henry Newbolt against Pound! All the same, there is by and large a crucial difference here between British and American attitudes, and one that is today every bit as marked as it was in 1912. For on nearly every American campus there is an atelier in the shape of a "Creative Writing program," whereas on no British campus is there any such thing, and indeed the British scoff at the mere possibility—on precisely the grounds that Newbolt here puts forward.

Pound's exasperated bewilderment before the spectacle of British loyalty to the amateur, and British readiness to pay the price in tolerance of the amateurish, is nowhere so evident as in his lifelong esteem for Laurence Binyon, the editor of the Hewlett *Letters*.

According to Noel Stock's *Life*, Pound first met Binyon in the second week of February 1909, and early in March he found "intensely interesting" a lecture by Binyon on European and Oriental art, for which the lecturer had sent him a ticket. Some time that year there occurred a famous meeting at the Vienna Cafe, in New Oxford Street near the British Museum, when Pound as Binyon's "bulldog" met Wyndham Lewis as the "bulldog" of T. Sturge Moore. This, nearly forty years later, was celebrated in canto 80:

> Mr Lewis had been to Spain
> Mr Binyon's young prodigies
> pronounced the word: Penthesilea
> There were mysterious figures
> that emerged from recondite recesses
> and ate at the WIENER CAFÉ
> which died into banking, Jozefff may have followed
> his emperor.
> "It is the sons pent up within a man"
> mumbled old Neptune
> "Laomedon, Ahi, Laomedon"
> or rather three "ahis" before the "Laomedon"
> "He stood" wrote Mr Newbolt, later Sir Henry
> "the door behind" and now they complain of cummings.
> So it is to Mr Binyon that I owe, initially.
> Mr Lewis, Mr P. Wyndham Lewis. His bull-dog, me,
> as it were against old Sturge M's bull-dog,

> Mr T. Sturge Moore's
>   bull-dog, et
>   meum est propositum, it is my intention
> in tabernam, or was, to the Wiener cafe
> you cannot yet buy one dish of Chinese food in all Italy
> hence the debacle
> "forloyn" said Mr Bridges (Robert)
> "we'll get 'em all back"
> meaning archaic words. . . .
>
> [506: 540]

For "prodigies" ("Mr Binyon's young prodigies") surely we ought to read "protégés"; and then it becomes possible to wonder whether the jocularity about bulldogs doesn't mask a wistful or resentful sense that Binyon and Sturge Moore ("old Neptune") might have done more with their respective protégés than merely set them to sniff and snarl at each other's heels; to question whether the two senior writers could not have established themselves—at least for some purposes—as masters of *ateliers* in which the two young hopefuls might have enrolled as apprentices. Instead, the outcome of what seems to have been an uncomfortable occasion was merely that Pound and Lewis took that much longer to find out that they were natural allies.

It was probably on this occasion that Binyon said something that Pound, misdating the event 1908, recalled in the postscript to a letter to Binyon in 1934:

> I wonder if you are using (in lectures) a statement I remember you making in talk, but not so far as I can recall, in print. "Slowness is beauty", which struck me as very odd in 1908 (when I certainly did not believe it) and has stayed with me ever since—shall we say as proof that you violated British habit; and thought of it.

Who thought of it? Binyon, or Pound? Hugh Kenner is no doubt right to suppose that it was Pound who had been thinking of it. For it crops up in the *Rock-Drill* canto 87, in the 1950s:

> Only sequoias are slow enough.
> BinBin "is beauty."
> "Slowness is beauty."
> [572:608]

The mingled exasperation and admiration that Pound felt for Binyon are nowhere so explicit and appealing as in what he wrote for *Blast* (July, 1915), so as to introduce into that inappropriately vociferous context nine quotations from the demure prose of Binyon's *The Flight of the Dragon. An Essay on the Theory and Practice of Art in China and Japan* (London, 1911):

We regret that we cannot entitle this article "Homage to Mr Lawrence (sic) Binyon," for Mr Binyon has not sufficiently rebelled. Manifestly he is not one of the ignorant. He is far from being one of the outer world, but in reading his work we constantly feel the influence upon him of his reading of the worst English poets. We find him in a disgusting attitude of respect toward predecessors whose intellect is vastly inferior to his own. This is loathesome (sic). Mr Binyon has thought; he has plunged into the knowledge of the East and extended the borders of occidental knowledge, and yet his mind constantly harks back to some folly of nineteenth century Europe. We can see him as it were constantly restraining his inventiveness, constantly trying to conform to an orthodox view against which his thoughts and emotions rebel, constantly trying to justify Chinese intelligence by dragging it a little nearer to some Western precedent. Ah well Mr Binyon has, indubitably, his moments. Very few men do have any moments whatever, and for the benefit of such readers as have not sufficiently respected Mr Binyon for his, it would be well to set forth a few of them. They are found in his "Flight of the Dragon", a book otherwise unpleasantly marred by his recurrent respect for inferior, very inferior people.

It isn't hard to see here, once again, Pound's baffled exasperation that, instead of setting up shop as *maître d'école*, "the very learned British Museum assistant" should resolutely duck back into doing such a worthy and humane but undoubtedly over-modest activity as editing such of the letters of his old friend Hewlett as could not conceivably give offense. Yet Binyon knew the unformulated rules of the society that he moved in, and played the game consistently as the amateur that that society required him to be. It is true to this day in England that, if one has learning, one must wear it so lightly that it is unnoticeable.

It would be tedious to quote and consider every one of the tributes that Pound paid to Binyon. One is at the end of *Gaudier-Brzeska* (1916); another is in a *Criterion* article of 1937, "D'Artagnan Twenty Years After"; in that year appeared *Polite Essays*, which includes Pound's review of Binyon's translation of the *Inferno* (originally in *The Criterion* for April 1934); there are two tributes to Binyon in *Guide to Kulchur* (1938); in 1948 at St. Elizabeth's Pound was still pressing Binyon on the attention of Charles Olson; and as late as 1958 he took the opportunity of *Pavannes and Divagations* to get back into print his appreciative note on *The Flight of the Dragon*.

None of these items is without interest. But "Hell," the review of Binyon's *Inferno*, is particularly important; for it may well be one of the most careful and illuminating acts of criticism that Pound ever performed. It includes this passage:

> I do not expect to see another version as good as Binyon's. . . . Few men of Binyon's position and experience have tried or will try the experiment. You cannot counterfeit forty years' honest work, or get the same result by being a clever

young man who prefers vanilla to orange or heliotrope to lavender perfume.

"La sculpture n'est pas pour les jeunes hommes."
(Brancusi)

A younger generation, or at least a younger American generation, has been brought up on a list of acid tests, invented to get rid of the boiled oatmeal consistency of the bad verse of 1900, and there is no doubt that many young readers seeing Binyon's inversions, etc., will be likely to throw down the translation under the impression that it is incompetent.

The fact that this idiom, which was never spoken on sea or land, is NOT fit for use in the new poetry of 1933-4 does not mean that it is unfit for use in a translation of a poem finished in 1321.

Pound may be right or wrong about the merits of Binyon's version, as about the sorts of language that are acceptable in verse translation; what is certain is that he's here applying to diction a sort of sliding scale or set of variable standards such as Ford's principles didn't allow for.

At any rate, Pound's enthusiasm for Binyon's version had led him to reopen correspondence with Binyon. And a letter of 30 August 1934 is particularly interesting, since it is rather plainly a reply to protests from Binyon about Pound's contemptuous treatment of Rubens. Pound's humility under Binyon's supposed rebuke is very striking:

Dear L. B: When one has finally done the job and found the *mot juste*, I dare say violent language usually disappears. Rubens' technique (at least in one painting about 4 ft. square) is not stupid. I dare say I damned him, for the whole grovelling imbecility of French court life from the

death of Francois Premier to the last fat slob that was guillo-
tined. . . . And my use of "idiotic" is loose. You are quite
right about that. Have always been interested in intelligence,
escaped the germy epoch of Freud and am so bored with *all*
lacks of intelletto that I haven't used any discrimination
when I have referred to 'em. . . .

If, as I'm inclined to believe, this unwonted willingness
to kiss the rod represents one last offer by Pound (at this
time, aged forty-eight!) to enroll in Binyon's seminar if
Binyon would only call it into being, Binyon once again
knew better than to understand what Pound was driving
at.

Oddly enough, the last word—though a mournful one—
can be with Maurice Hewlett. For in 1920, when Binyon
began work towards his version of the *Inferno*, he ex-
changed letters with Hewlett, who had translated the first
canto years before, and now urged Binyon to shorten
his measure to tetrameters, pointing out that this was
what he himself had done in his "Song of the Plow," a
long poem in terza rima in which he had invested a great
deal. Hewlett remarked: "Another thing: putting in
eights compels the terseness of Dante, wh. amounts
sometimes to a vice in him. Still, there it is, and you
must reproduce it." How could Binyon have failed to re-
member this, when Pound complimented him by saying,
"He has carefully preserved all the faults of his original"?
In *Guide to Kulchur* (chapter 30) Pound was to say, again
with Binyon's translation specifically in mind, "Honest
work has its reward in the arts if no other where." How
one would like that to be true! But turning over the
pages of poor Hewlett's unreadable but honest "Song of
the Plow," one wonders about that. One does indeed.

EZRA POUND ABANDONS THE ENGLISH

Ezra Pound's long love affair with England, and his angry and wounded turning against her in 1917 or 1918, cannot of course bulk so large in an American's sense of him as in an Englishman's. It is an American, Herbert Schniedau, who has asked:

> Can any man who identifies himself with the British world of letters, however independent and tolerant he may be, write a fair-minded book about Pound? What Pound did to English literature and British sensibilities doesn't seem forgivable, and I really think that the English were more offended by Pound's political obsessions than were the countrymen he ostensibly betrayed.

This is fair comment; and the last clause in particular is, surprisingly, manifestly true, explain it how we may.

And yet an Englishman's relation to English culture and its traditions may be more tormented than Schniedau allows for, especially if the Englishman in question defines himself as, or aspires to be, an English *artist*. Such a one may feel that Pound's "writing off" of England, his abandonment of her—physically in 1920, in imagination some years earlier—was abundantly justified, to the extent indeed that it was not so much his justified rejection of her, as *her* unjustifiable rejection of *him*. And yet such an Englishman must wonder: Was there once virtue in England, which subsequently went out of her? If so, when did this happen? In the casualty lists from the Battle of the Somme? (Or is that merely rhetoric?) And can the virtue that thus went out of the spiritual

---

This article first appeared in *Poetry Nation* (Manchester, England), no. 4 (1975).

reality called England ever be restored? Has there been such a restoration, since 1920? If so, when did it happen? And if not, when will it ever happen? When, and how?

These are serious and painful questions. At all events there are Englishmen who find them so. To take one example out of many, the native Englishman D. H. Lawrence reached just the same conclusion as Pound at just the same time, and Lawrence's letters record it; he concluded, just as Pound did, that England after the First World War was, for the artist, uninhabitable. The names of Robert Graves, W. H. Auden, and Christopher Isherwood may serve to remind us of English writers who seem to have reached the same dismaying conclusion over the years since.

However that may be, there are reasons for thinking that the abandonment of England, and of any hopes for her, was not much less momentous for Pound than it is for his English readers. After all, Pound had *married* England—not figuratively, but literally, in the person of Dorothy Shakespear; and Ben Hecht in 1918 reported that Pound was "a doting monogamist".[1] It didn't last; his alienation from England seems to have coincided with an alienation from Dorothy, for within five years he had a child by Olga Rudge. And this is not altogether surprising; for Dorothy Pound seems to have been English in a singularly entire and uncompromising fashion. The daughter of Olivia Shakespear, who had been briefly Yeats's mistress and had bought Wyndham Lewis's canvases and Gaudier's drawings, Dorothy told Hugh Kenner in 1965, "I read poetry only with difficulty. I never did much care for it."[2] She said also, recalling Pound translating Noh plays on their honeymoon at Stone Cottage in Sussex, "I was not then preoccupied with plays and characters. I was trying to make out what sort of creature I was going to be living with." Moreover, Dorothy's

Englishness was centuries old: among her cousins was one Charles Talbot—"one of the Shakespear names," she said—who owned a medieval abbey, "and once Ezra and I crawled over the roof to a turret to see a copy of the Magna Charta, kept there in a glass case." In 1945, in an American prison camp near Pisa, Pound remembered that (canto 80):

> To watch a while from the tower
>> where dead flies lie thick over the old charter
> forgotten, oh quite forgotten
> but confirming John's first one,
>> and still there if you climb over attic rafters;
> to look at the fields; are they tilled?
> is the old terrace alive as it might be
> with a whole colony
>> if money be free again?
> Chesterton's England of has-been and why-not,
> or is it all rust, ruin, death duties and mortgages
> and the great carriage yard empty
>> and more pictures gone to pay taxes
>> When a dog is tall but
>> not so tall as all that
>> that dog is a Talbot
>>> (a bit long in the pasterns?)
> When a butt is ½ as tall as a whole butt
> That butt is a small butt
>> Let backe and side go bare
> and the old kitchen left as the monks had left it
> and the rest as time has cleft it.
>
> (Only shadows enter my tent
>> as men pass between me and the sunset). . .

If, as Hugh Kenner believes, Pound never ceased to love Dorothy even while he loved Olga, this is surely part of what he loved in her, an aspect of what she meant to him; and so Pound's feelings for and about England were, right to the end, not much less tormented than any

English reader's can be. And the English reader who does not understand that the punning on "Talbot" is painful and all but hysterical, like the punning of Shakespeare's Hamlet, does not understand Pound at all. As for Dorothy's loyalty, it proved equal to any occasion; and in particular through the years of Pound's incarceration in St. Elizabeth's her devotion was exemplary. Certainly she was no philistine, but a graphic artist herself. And yet . . . "I read poetry only with great difficulty. I never did much care for it." It is at any rate possible that in her a certain ethical rightness and decency coexisted with aesthetic stiffness and suspicion. It was a not uncommon combination in a certain breed of Englishman and Englishwoman—a breed perhaps now vanished, which is not to say, improved upon.

As for canto 80, it continues, and closes upon, "the matter of England":

beyond the eastern barbed wire
   a sow with nine boneen
matronly as any duchess at Claridge's
and for that Christmas at Maurie Hewlett's
Going out from Southampton
they passed the car by the dozen
     who would not have shown weight on a scale
        riding, riding
           for Noel the green holly
   Noel, Noel, the green holly
   A dark night for the holly

That would have been Salisbury plain,
   and I have not thought of
     the Lady Anne for this twelve years
       Nor of Le Portel
How tiny the panelled room where they stabbed him
       In her lap, almost, La Stuarda
     Si tuit li dolh ehl planh el marrimen
       for the leopards and broom plants

Tudor indeed is gone and every rose,
Blood-red, blanch-white that in the sunset glows
Cries: 'Blood, Blood, Blood!' against the gothic stone
Of England, as the Howard or Boleyn knows.

Nor seeks the carmine petal to infer;
Nor is the white bud Time's inquisitor
Probing to know if its new-gnarled root
Twists from York's head or belly of Lancaster;

Or if a rational soul should stir, perchance,
Within the stem or summer shoot to advance
Contrition's utmost throw, seeking in thee
But oblivion, not thy forgiveness, FRANCE.

as the young lizard extends his leopard spots
    along the grass-blade seeking the green midge
        half an ant-size
and the Serpentine will look just the same
and the gulls be as neat on the pond
and the sunken garden unchanged
and God knows what else is left of our London
        my London, your London
and if her green elegance
    remains on this side of my rain ditch
    puss lizard will lunch on some other T-bone

sunset grand couturier.

"That Christmas" (not that it matters) was Christmas 1911, which Pound spent as a guest of Maurice Hewlett's at the Old Rectory, Broad Chalke, Salisbury—a house which had once been a nunnery, dating back to 1487.[3] Driving with Hewlett across Thomas Hardy's Wessex, the scene is peopled for Pound with the ghosts of rustic waits and mummers of the long English past, such as those of Hardy's *Under the Greenwood Tree*, one of Pound's favorite books. Hewlett, author of *The Queen's Quair*, brings to mind another writer who had similarly concerned himself with Mary Queen of Scots ("La Stuarda")—that is to say, Swinburne in his *Mary Stuart*. Swinburne is alluded to, here as elsewhere, by the place-name "Le Portel," where—so Pound seems to have believed (wrongly, for the name is "Yport")—Swinburne on a famous occasion was saved from drowning by French fishermen. At Holyrood House in Edinburgh one is still shown the room where Rizzio was stabbed "in her lap almost." The line in Provençal is from Bertran de Born's "Planh for the Young English King," which Pound had translated splendidly as early as 1909. The "leopards and broom plants," Plantagenet emblems, signify the dynastic reasons for which Henry the young king was killed, as were Rizzio and Mary's husband Darnley centuries later.

Anyone is free to decide that life is too short for such unriddlings; others (I speak from experience) may develop a taste for them. A more important point is that passages of this sort, spliced as they are with images like the lizard from the immediate foreground of Pound's tent inside the wire-mesh cage of the prison camp, do not come into being out of the free associations of idle reverie, though in these Pisan cantos Pound exploits the illusion of that, as Joyce did in *Ulysses* when he pretended to transport himself and us into the mind of Leopold Bloom. The reason we are reminded of these historical episodes, rather than any of a hundred others, comes clear only with the surprising and congested line that closes the quatrains about the Wars of the Roses: "But oblivion, not thy forgiveness, FRANCE." The England that Pound mourns the loss of is, as it had been for him from the first, an integral province of western Europe, sharing a common culture with France and always reaching out, through France, to the shores of the Mediterranean.

This emphasis will not commend itself to the English reader whom Herbert Schniedau envisages. Such a reader is likely to define his Englishness as precisely that which continental Europe is not. And in fact, of recent years Dickens's Mr. Podsnap has walked again, cherishing insularity as a patriotic duty. But of course there are other things in this passage which will put English teeth on edge. Colonel Blimp today is likely to be a Roundhead colonel, in his professed sentiments a Leveller, though not of course in his practices. And his egalitarianism will be offended by "the great carriage yard empty," and by "more pictures gone to pay taxes." Especially as voiced by an American who had disloyally taken the wrong side in a war just successfully completed "for democracy," the sentiments must have seemed—in 1948, when *The Pisan Cantos* appeared—nothing short of shameless! An English writer who went into self-exile just when Pound and Lawrence did, Ford Madox Ford, had always been denied serious consideration (as he is denied it still), in part for having, in *No More Parades* at the end of a previous war, envisaged the England he was leaving in just such manorial terms; and if the Englishman could not be forgiven, how forgive the American? (Lawrence, it is true, envisaged the England *he* was relinquishing very largely in the image of Garsington Manor; but then, Lawrence's origins are so impeccably proletarian that the aberration can be overlooked!)

And then there is the insolence of the last line: "sunset grand couturier." Isn't that the giveaway? It will certainly seem so to the Englishman (as I take him to be), who found in the "Envoi" to *Hugh Selwyn Mauberley*—Pound's most explicit farewell to England, as he prepared to leave her in 1918—"externality: an externality which, considering what *Mauberley* attempts, is utterly disabling."[4] This is the same reader who, having decided that the "Envoi" is *"literary*, in a limiting sense," is provoked by the word "magic" in the middle stanza into deciding that "the term 'literary' becomes a good deal more limiting, for the term 'aesthetic' rises to our lips, and so, perhaps, does 'American.'" And there we have it! For this sort of Englishman, "externality"—to things English—is what any American is condemned to; and per contra "inwardness"—with things English—is what an Englishman quite simply has, painlessly, as a birthright. From this point of view, the only good American is one who stays shamefacedly mute about his English cousins, however many years he may have lived among them. The same rule does not hold, it will be noticed, when there is any question of Englishmen talking about Americans.

The comment I have been quoting from appeared in 1965. The vocabulary is different from the comments of fifty years earlier which wounded and infuriated Pound, and drove him out of England,[5] but the sentiments are identical. And indeed even the vocabulary is sometimes the same. The horrifying thing about, for instance, Robert Nichols's review in the *Observer* for 11 January 1920—"Mr. Pound, indeed, serves his lobster à l'Américaine"—is that it could perfectly well have appeared in the *Observer* last Sunday.

It is entirely possible to think that if "literary" and "aesthetic" are words that go naturally with "American" but not with "English," so much the worse for the English. Ah, but we mean "literary"—presumably "aesthetic" also—"in a limiting sense." Yet from those English lips which utter this face-saving locution, one has yet to hear the words uttered in any sense that is *not* "limiting." And from a set of preconceptions like that there is no way into Pound's universe at all. As regards "externality," for instance, Pound may be thought to admit the charge, and to glory in it. For he applauded

Wyndham Lewis's alter ego in *Tarr*, when the latter explained that it is a condition of art "*to have no* inside, nothing you cannot see. It is not something impelled like a machine by a little egoistic inside"; and again, "deadness, in the limited sense in which we use that word, is the first condition of art. The second is absence of *soul*, in the sentimental human sense. The lines and masses of a statue are its soul."[6] Between a *limiting* sense (for "literary") and a *limited* sense (for "deadness"), we are here navigating in light and tricky airs. And Pound had later to explain what he meant, and what he did *not* mean, by his endorsement of Lewis. After all, he was later to applaud Hardy's poetry for having precisely, "the insides." Yet he never retracted this avowal; nor—given what he meant by it—did he need to. The clue to what he meant is the last sentence from Lewis: "The lines and masses of a statue are its soul." That "inwardness" so prized by some English readers, and characteristically found by them (implausibly) in Lawrence, is an attention directed so far "inward" that it can never come to the surface for long enough to notice how the sunlight breaks upon the edges and volumes of a piece of sculpture; and that is why indeed such readers cannot use the word "aesthetic" except "in a limiting sense."

Accordingly, the most instructive gloss on "externality" is to be found where we might expect, in Pound's 1916 memoir of the sculptor, Gaudier-Brzeska, where he writes of Gaudier and Lewis and other "vorticists," painters, and sculptors:

> These new men have made me see form, have made me more conscious of the sky where it juts down between houses, of the bright pattern of sunlight which the bath water throws up on the ceiling, of the great "Vs" of light that dart through the chinks over the curtain rings, all these are new chords, new keys of design.

It is in this profoundly grateful and reverent sense, certainly not with any heartless flippancy, that forty years later in the prison stockade Pound greets the sunset as a designer—"grand couturier." Plainly the man who wrote this was the man who in *Hugh Selwyn Mauberley* took as his model and master Gautier, who described himself proudly as a man "pour qui le monde visible existe." But the English reader has a label ready to tie on to Theophile Gautier; and by this time we can guess what is written on it—"arid aestheticism."[7]

When Schniedau says, "What Pound did to English literature and British sensibilities doesn't seem forgivable," he doubtless has in mind certain passages from *How to Read*, which was originally addresssed to the American readers of the *New York Herald Tribune Books* on 13, 20, and 27 January 1929. For instance:

> The Britons never have shed barbarism; they are proud to tell you that Tacitus said the last word about Germans. When Mary Queen of Scots went to Edinburgh she bewailed going out among savages, and she herself went from a sixteenth-century court that held but a barbarous, or rather a drivelling and idiotic and superficial travesty of the Italian culture as it had been before the debacle of 1527. The men who tried to civilize these shaggy and uncouth marginalians by bringing them news of civilization have left a certain number of translations that are better reading today than are the works of the ignorant islanders who were too proud to translate.

Whereupon Pound applauds, as he had done before and was to do again, Gavin Douglas's translation of Virgil and Arthur Golding's and Marlowe's translations of Ovid. Again (where Pound's addressing himself to Americans is especially evident):

> We are so encumbered by having British literature in our foreground that . . . one must speak of it in disproportion.

It was kept alive during the last century by a series of exotic injections. Swinburne read Greek and took English metric in hand; Rossetti brought in the Italian primitives; Fitzgerald made the only good poem of the time that has gone to the people; it is called, and is to a great extent, a translation or mistranslation.

There was a faint waft of early French influence. Morris translated sagas, the Irish took over the business for a few years; Henry James led, or rather preceded, the novelists, and then the Britons resigned *en bloc*; the language is now in the keeping of the Irish (Yeats and Joyce); apart from Yeats, since the death of Hardy, poetry is being written by Americans. All the developments in English verse since 1910 are due almost wholly to Americans. In fact, there is no longer any reason to call it English verse, and there is no present reason to think of England at all.

This is unfair? Yes, of course it is. Elsewhere in *How to Read* Pound remembers Landor and Browning, and has to make special provision to exempt them from these strictures. Moreover, when Pound revised and expanded *How to Read*, to make *ABC of Reading* (1934), he obliquely admitted the unfairness of these passages. But they are not *manifestly* unfair; there is a case to answer. We English have never answered the case, because we have refused to recognize that the case was ever made. And so the case against us has gone by default. Among serious writers and readers in the United States (as distinct from shallow and modish Anglophiles mostly around New York), it is taken for granted that Pound's caustic dismissal of us in 1929 was justified, and that nothing has happened in the forty-five years since to alter that picture significantly. Hugh Kenner, for instance, in a work of massive scholarship, *The Pound Era* (1971), can write: "By the mid-1920s a massive triviality, a failure of will on a truly forbidding scale, was allowing English culture to lapse into shapes characterized by childishness, self-indulgence, utter predictability." And throughout Kenner's book "English" is taken to imply arrogant obtuseness, complacent inertia, and effeminate enervation. If we resent this (as we should), we ought to realize that it is we who are to blame for it. For neither Kenner nor Pound is a professional or obsessive Anglophobe. Both men are reporting what seem to them the facts of the case, and they are the more confident about doing so because no Englishman has arisen to rebut their arguments. For us to respond with sneering anti-Americanism is the merest childishness.

After this, Pound's relations with England and the English were for the most part an aspect of his relations with that one of his erstwhile protégés who had become, surprisingly, a pillar of the English establishment—Eliot, editor of the *Criterion*. And these negotiations are mostly conducted in a tone of high comedy; after 1930 Pound's anger is virtually monopolized by Roosevelt's U.S.A., and English culture is for him just something that he can't take seriously. This does not prevent him from honoring English writing when it is honorable; for instance Binyon's Dante, Rouse's Homer, the early books of Adrian Stokes, and the poems of Basil Bunting. But the preferred tone is one of indulgent banter. (And at the risk of laboring the obvious, let it be said that Pound is often a very *funny* writer, in verse and prose alike.) If the English reader doesn't like this, let him ask himself if Housman's *Name and Nature of Poetry*, or—touching as it is, and as Pound acknowledges—the career of Harold Monro, is not treated with as much compassionate indulgence as possible in the *Criterion* articles by Pound which he reprinted in *Polite Essays* (1937).

Still more to the point is another essay in that volume, "Mr. Eliot's Solid Merit" (originally in the *New English Weekly* for 12 July 1934). Considering that this was written at a time when Pound's reputation was eclipsed as Eliot's rose towards the zenith, the generosity of this essay, its lack of rancor, is admirable. And Pound's generosity towards Eliot did not fail through subsequent decades, when nothing was more common among the English intelligentsia, especially the academic part of it, than to assail Pound with weapons picked from Eliot's armory. This strategy is still in high favor among us. It consists of making categorical and systematic certain distinctions made, and preferences expressed, by Eliot in his essays; and then dismissing Pound merely because he writes with a measure of respect of certain writers (Swinburne is one example) on whom Eliot, the arbiter of taste, is supposed to have conclusively turned down his thumbs. At its most ludicrous, this makes the "Envoi" to *Hugh Selwyn Mauberley* suspect, or worse than suspect, simply because it alludes to Edmund Waller, whereas the okay authors from Waller's period, among pedestrian readers of Eliot's essays, are taken to be Donne and Marvell. Eliot, needless to say, never countenanced these devious maneuvers.

We should now be in a position to answer Herbert Schniedau's question: "Can any man who identifies himself with the British world of letters . . . write a fair-minded book about Pound?" The answer is: Yes, this can be done, and it *has been* done—by G. S. Fraser, for one. If the English writer stops short of uncritical adulation, and also has a longer memory than the Americans for the loathsome politics that Pound was infected by, that is all to the good. There *are* British Poundians, and they are among the best. If there are few of them, we have seen why. It is because trying to give credit to this great poet commits a patriotic Englishman (or Scotsman for that matter—Fraser is a Scot) to very tormenting and unwelcome questions and reflections about the spiritual state of England or Scotland today, and over the last fifty years. It is therefore inevitable that our Poundians will be exceptions, and that majority opinion for the foreseeable future will be more or less hysterically hostile to Pound. This would not matter so much if Pound had not been a great technical innovator in verse writing. Because the British world of letters as a whole has refused, and still refuses, to consider Pound temperately, it refuses to acknowledge—indeed, it cannot even *understand*—the poetic forms that Pound invented, or the principles of form which he enunciated. And in saying this, one has in mind not the *Cantos* but the much more straightforward and generally serviceable forms which Pound put into currency in collections like *Ripostes* (1912) and *Lustra* (1916). One thinks, for instance, of imagism, and of the treatment which the TLS meted out to Peter Jones's anthology of imagist poetry. In short, what happens is that in England—and here one *does* mean England, rather than Scotland or Ireland—the nonacademic makers and molders of literary opinion are judging poetry by standards which are sixty years out-of-date. The rest of the world surveys this spectacle with amused disbelief.

Notes

1. Quoted by W. K. Rose, "Pound and Lewis: the Crucial Years," in *Agenda* Wyndham Lewis Special Issue (1969-70), p. 130.
2. Hugh Kenner, "D. P. Remembered," *Paideuma* 2, no. 3 (1973), pp. 486-93.
3. Noel Stock, *The Life of Ezra Pound* (London, 1970), p. 108.
4. A. L. French, "Olympian Apathein . . ." in *Essays in Criticism* (1965). Reprinted in *Ezra Pound: A Critical Anthology*, ed. J. P. Sullivan (Penguin, 1970), pp. 326-42.
5. See particularly the last pages of "Remy de Gourmont: A Distinction," (in Pound, *Instigations*, 1920). Here we find quoted G. W. Prothero of *The Quarterly Review* in 1914 refusing to print Pound in those august pages because of Pound's association with the Vorticist magazine, *Blast*—"It stamps a man too

disadvantageously." More strikingly, a letter from de Gourmont in 1915 wonders none too politely if his writings could ever be acceptable to American readers; and Pound reproducing the letter reflects tartly that they certainly couldn't be acceptable to the English!

6. Pound, *Instigations*, p. 223.
7. A. L. French, "Olympian Apathein . . ." in *Essays in Criticism* (1965). Reprinted in *Ezra Pound: A Critical Anthology*, ed. J. P. Sullivan (Penguin, 1970), pp. 326-42.

POUND AND *THE EXILE*

If we look at Pound in 1927 and 1928, when he instituted from or through Paris his periodical, *The Exile,* and sustained it through four issues, we get the impression of a man yawing about without direction, as at no time either earlier or later in his career. The very pages of his own magazine express the discernibly patronizing indulgence that it seems the American expatriate community extended to him. Robert McAlmon, writing reportage in *The Exile* number 2, noted: "At the Stryx, I found Ezra Pound talking to an English girl, and describing America as it never was, is not, and never will be. I was glad to see Ezra, because what biased attitudes he has are so biased that he manages to be, all round, a more generous-minded and discriminating person than others who spread their capacity for bias over their entire mental outlook." This is certainly not the language that one uses of a resident sage or recognized "master"; and it seems that in Paris at that time there was in fact no one who esteemed Pound in either of those ways.

For just this reason the issues of *The Exile,* though they provide only conflicting evidence about Pound's acumen as an editor, are very instructive about the cast of his sensibility. Particularly interesting is the fact that, after backing so many winners, Pound in *The Exile* backed unmistakably at least one loser. This was Ralph Cheever Dunning, whose "Threnody in Sapphics" appeared in *The Exile* number 2, and was strenuously defended by Pound in number 3:

My present feeling is that any one who cannot feel the beauty of their melody had better confine his criticism to prose and leave the discussion of verse to those who understand something about it. . . . It still seems to me that the acting critics of poesy are for the most part incapable of looking for more than one thing at a time, having got started about 1913 (I mean a few of 'em got started about 1913 and a lot have started since) to look for a certain plainness and directness of speech and simple order of words; and having about 1918 got started looking for Mr Eliot's rather more fragile system (a system excellent for Mr Eliot but not very much use to any one else), they now limit their criticism to inquiring whether or no verse conforms to one or other of these manners, thereby often omitting to notice fundamentals, or qualities as important as verbal directness and even more important than "snap."

The meaning of "snap" in relation to Eliot's "rather more fragile system" is at this date, I suppose, irrecoverable; but the general drift of these remarks is clear.

And this is not the only place in *The Exile* where Pound shows himself restive inside the image of himself that had been built up among initiates by his propaganda of fifteen years before, when he had taken over "imagism" and championed Ford Madox Ford's ideas about a diction for poetry that should be "plain" and "direct." At the end of this same issue of *The Exile* there appears from Pound a page headed "Desideria":

Quite simply: I want a new civilization. We have the basis for a new poetry, and for a new music.

But this ringing declaration is no sooner issued than it has to be qualified virtually out of existence. In the first place,

> I say "new" civilization, I don't know that I *care* about its being so very different from the best that has been, but it must be *as good* as the best that has been.

And secondly, much more to our present purposes:

> (Parenthesis. No, dearie, when I say, the basis for a new poetry, I don't mean the vers libre movement as it was in the year 1912.)

Of course the most cursory glance at Dunning's "Threnody in Sapphics" (not to speak of more miserable performances like "Isabelle of Hainault" in *The Exile* number 3) shows that Pound had, as it were, no alternative; there was no way to vindicate Dunning by imagist principles. He could not be vindicated by any other principles, either. But before we jump to the conclusion that Pound had simply had a brainstorm, or had been trapped by misplaced compassion for Dunning as a lame duck, we ought to consider another possibility—that imagism, and Pound's endorsement of Ford's insistence on "the prose tradition," had never been for him more than an aberration, though in the short term a very profitable one, from a way of feeling that impelled him always toward the *cantabile*, a proclivity that would, in the interests of melody, tolerate notably eccentric diction. It is thus that he declares himself for Dunning's sapphics, flashing out at "any one who cannot feel the beauty of their *melody*" (my italics). And within six years, wanting to register (in *The Criterion* for 1934) the distinction of Binyon's version of the *Inferno* despite its consistent inversions of prosaic word order, Pound found himself in the same situation, having to contend with those who had learned too well or too inflexibly the lessons he himself had taught them:

> Before flying to the conclusion that certain things are "against the rules" (heaven save us, procedures are already erected into RULES!) let the neophyte consider that a man cannot be in New York and Pekin at the same moment. Certain qualities are in OPPOSITION to others, water cannot exist as water and as ice at the same time.

Moreover these were the years when Pound was writing canto 30:

> Compleynt, compleynt I hearde upon a day,
> Artemis singing, Artemis, Artemis
> Agaynst Pity lifted her wail:
> Pity causeth the forests to fail,
> Pity slayeth my nymphs . . .

and canto 36:

> I have no will to try proof-bringing
> Or say where it hath birth
> What is its virtu and power
> Its being and every moving
> Or delight whereby tis called "to love"
> Or if man can show it to sight.

To be sure, both of these cantos are special cases—as was, we may suppose, the "Envoi" to *Hugh Selwyn Mauberley*, written many years before. Yet in one sense the circumstances of any and every poem are "special"; and at any rate all these instances show that, in his own writing as in the writing of others, Pound was prepared to recognize circumstances which justified departing very far indeed from Ford's and the imagists' precepts about diction, indeed flying in the face of them.

But what, then, are we to make of it when, in 1939, writing an obituary of Ford, Pound lumped together two old associates of his, Fred Manning and Henry Newbolt, and excoriated them for continuing to use the "poetical" diction from which Ford's timely polemics had weaned Pound himself? Is this inconsistency? Is it worse—positive dishonesty? And what's to be said of his declaration, as late as 1964 (in *Confucius to Cummings*, the anthology he put together with Marcella Spann), that Ford's insistence on "the limpidity of natural speech, driven towards the just word, not slopping down . . . into the more ordinary Wordsworthian word" was "the most important critical act of the half-century"? How could Pound continue to proclaim this, when his own writing for decades before had belied it? (For undeniably, the cantos are not *limpid*; much of them isn't "speech" at all, but "song"; and of the parts that are speech, by no means all are "natural.") Have we convicted Pound of inconsistency, or worse?

I think not. Pound knew enough of his own gifts, and of the protracted strenuousness of his apprenticeship, to know that what was safe for him was not safely available to others, least of all to those he called "the neophyte." He knew too that the poem he was engaged upon, *The Cantos,* was unprecedented and (he must have thought) *sui generis.* (He was not to know that Charles Olson, after next to no apprenticeship at all, would recklessly try to emulate him.) But in any case, the best proof of the pudding is in the eating—by which I mean that any one who has tried to help young poets over the years, whether in Britain or America, knows that Ford's and the imagists' precepts about diction are what most of them most need to learn—no novelty, after all, since they can learn the same lessons from the preface to *Lyrical Ballads*, if they choose to. What they learn in such a case is, of course, only a rule of thumb; for if criticism sometimes has to be prescriptive, its prescriptions are never applicable except "by and large." Rules of thumb are the only rules there are, in the *atelier*. But experience has taught me that this is the rule of thumb that can be most profitably proposed and acted upon. I dare to go further: some of the most gifted and earnest among my contemporaries—I think of Edgar Bowers in the United States and Geoffrey Hill in the United Kingdom (though I except Hill's wonderful *Mercian Hymns*)—fall short of pleasing me as they might, because they seem not to have followed this rule of thumb, and their language is habitually for my taste a shade, or several shades, too grandiloquent or "literary." I conclude that Ford's "critical act" was indeed (by and large, always by and large) the most important of the first half of this century, and that it is, moreover, irreversible.

SICILY IN *THE CANTOS*

When was Pound in Sicily? How many visits did he pay to the island? What particular cities and districts did he visit? For which of these excursions was he in the company of Yeats? Presumably from the Pound papers now at New Haven it would not be hard to come up with answers to these questions. But in the meantime the printed sources are hazy, if not quite contradictory. According to Noel Stock (*The Life of Ezra Pound* [1970], p. 251),

This article first appeared in *Paideuma* 6, no. 1 (1977).

"about the middle of February 1923 the Pounds went to Sicily with Yeats and his wife." On the other hand, in Joseph Hone's *W. B. Yeats, 1865-1939* (1942, p. 367) we read that the Yeatses went to Sicily in November 1924 and stayed for two months, "the attraction there being, besides the sunlight, the presence of Ezra Pound on the island, and the Byzantine mosaics of Monreale and the Capella Palatina at Palermo." Certainly Pound was writing from Taormina in December 1924, and writing to Joyce from Syracuse on 21 January 1925 (*Pound/Joyce,* ed. Forrest Read, 1967). And Richard Ellmann, in *New Approaches to Ezra Pound* (1969), names *1925* as the year in which the two poets, with their respective wives, were together in Sicily. All one can say with any certainty is that the Pounds (and probably the Yeatses also) paid at least two visits to Sicily in these years, and that on at least one occasion—probably on more than one—they stayed there for some weeks, if not months.

If we look in *The Cantos* for traces left by this experience, we are surprised to find how few they are, and how meager. We might think that "Naxos" in cantos 2, 24, and 78 is the place of that name beneath Taormina, the site (lately and partially excavated) of the earliest Greek colony in Sicily, and thereafter the port whence the teams from all the Sicilian Greek cities made a ceremonial departure to compete in the Olympic Games; but the *Annotated Index* is doubtless right to identify Naxos, on the contrary, with an island in the Aegean. Apart from that, we have (at 25/115) "that serene Lord King Frederic of Sicily"—which is to say, Frederick of Aragon (1272-1337), who was Frederick II, king of Sicily (1296-1337). At 27/129, we hear of "the earthquake in Messina" (28 December 1908), but this is merely incidental to the vast *blague* perpetrated by Romains, Vildrac, and others in Paris—to be nostalgically remembered years later in the Pisan canto 80 (see Richard Sieburth in *Paideuma* 2, p. 280). At 77/467 and again at 80/512, reference to the "quai" or "quais" at or of "Siracusa" seem not much less adventitious, in the sense that location in the Sicilian city of Syracuse seems, at first sight anyhow, not to be significant. Rather more arresting is 80/503:

> hurled into unstillness, Ixion
> Trinacrian manxman

—where "Trinacria," the ancient Greek name for Sicily, is related to the legend of how Vulcan the divine smith, somewhere in the island, solved the problem of perpetual motion by a wheel with three dogleg spokes, its never ceasing to roll recalling the wheel that was the hellish and interminable torment of Ixion. (The same three-spoked wheel is the heraldic emblem of the Isle of Man.) There remains the joke, at 82/524, on the name of Frederic W. Tancred, a member of the Hulme-Flint circle (ca. 1909), chiming with that of Tancred, Norman king of Sicily (d. 1194). This is a poor harvest from those weeks or months that the Pounds spent in Sicily; and indeed it is no harvest at all, since none of these allusions depends in any way on the poet's having been physically present in the island.

The same is true of a passage in the Rockdrill canto 94 (94/640-41):

> Acre, again,
>   with an Eleanor
> who sucked the venom out of his wound,
>   and came up via Padua,
> for a balance of wine & wool,
>   distraint and tolls not unbridled
> and in 1288 a thunderbolt passed between them

> this wd/be in the time of Federico Secondo,
> Alfonso, St. Louis, and Magnus of Norway
> and two years later she died and his luck went out,
> Edwardus, who played Baliol against the Bruce
> and brought the stone down to London
> where it is seen to this day
> PACTUM SERVA
> Be Traist.

Here the Sicilian reference, in itself a very slight one but worth pointing out for reasons that will emerge, is in "Federico Secondo," who is identical with the "Frederic" of canto 25, glossed above. It is essential not to confound him with the greater Frederick II (Hohenstaufen), holy Roman emperor from 1215 to 1250, and before that (1198-1212) king of Sicily as Frederick I. For this great figure, author of *The Book of the Falcon* and a hero for Dante as well as Pound, is to figure portentously in the Thrones cantos to come as we shall see. By the same token, we have to keep a watch on dates so as to see that this Eleanor is *not* Eleanor of Aquitaine, but her great-great-granddaughter, Eleanor of Castile, wife of Edward I of England. The possibility of confusion is very great; for just as Eleanor of Castile landed at Acre in 1270, accompanying Edward on the seventh crusade, so Eleanor of Aquitaine had landed there 120 years before, accompanying *her* husband (that is, her first, Louis VII of France) on *his* crusade—which is presumably what Pound means by "Acre, *again*." (This "rhyme in history" between namesakes is doubtless meant to strengthen the already well-established conflation of these Eleanors with their near namesakes, Helen of Troy and Helen of Tyre.) Most of the details about Eleanor and her relations with Edward, including his attempts to subjugate Scotland, symbolically signified by his removing the Stone of Scone to London, are found in the first volume of that small classic, Agnes Strickland's *Lives of the Queens of England* (1864).

At 97/681-2, we get:

PUER APULIUS

"Fresca rosa" sang Alcamo.
Of Antoninus very little record remains

That he wrote the book of the Falcon,
Mirabile brevitate correxit, says Landulph,
of Justinian's Code.

And here is the other Frederick, the Hohenstaufen emperor, he who wrote *The Book of the Falcon (The Art of Falconry, being the De Arte Venandi cum Avibus*, tr. C. A. Wood and F. Marjorie Fyfe, (1943). He appears under the name he was given in his orphaned youth—the Boy from Apulia. And with him comes Ciullo d'Alcamo, whose "Rosa Fresca aulentissima" was translated by D. G. Rossetti: "Thou sweetly-smelling fresh red rose / That near thy summer art. . . ." This poem, and its author, figure in *The Spirit of Romance*, as showing that Italian poetry taking up from Provence originated not in Tuscany but Sicily. Though Ciullo by Rossetti's reckoning composed the poem in the 1170s, at least twenty years before Frederick Hohenstaufen came to the throne of Sicily, Pound in *The Spirit of Romance* juxtaposes the two names, presumably as "an instigation"—though to what, it is not easy to say. Fifty years later, in *Thrones,* this is still the best that he can do—juxtaposing the two authors, and the two compositions, as here, so also at 98/689, 100/719, and 103/736. If significance is supposed to accrue with each repeated conjunction, it fails to do so for me.

However, at canto 106/753-54 (there is a brief allusion at 104/745 to the mosaics at Monreale), we do at last find a Sicilian allusion in the context of writing that we can recognize as distinguished:

> That the goddess turn crystal within her
> This is grain rite
>   Luigi in the hill path
>   this is grain rite
> near Enna, at Nyssa:
>   Circe, Persephone
> so different is sea from glen that
>   the juniper is her holy bush
> between the two pine trees, not Circe
>   but Circe was like that
>   coming from the house of smoothe stone
> "not know which god"
>   nor could enter her eyes by probing
>   the light blazed behind her
>   nor was this from sunset

Enna, traditional location of the rape of Persephone (see Milton), is in mid-Sicily. But the location is, as it were, accidental, and contributes nothing to the tension between Circe and Persephone as it has been teased out, in this passage along with others, by Guy Davenport (see his "Persephone's Ezra," in *New Approaches to Ezra Pound*).

In canto 107, the Sicilian references suddenly come quite thick and fast, spliced into numerous quotations from Sir Edward Coke. This makes sense to the degree that one of the legal authorities whom Coke most often cites is Bracton (Henry de Bracton, *De Legibus et Consuetudinibus Angliae*), who died in 1268, having flourished under Henry III of England and during the minority of Henry's son, the future Edward I. Moreover Edward and Eleanor spent the winter of 1270-71 in

Sicily, en route to the Holy Land, and returned there in 1272 for Edward to learn that, his father having died, he was king of England. These are frail reasons, but the best I can find, for canto 107 to begin with a flourish of Sicilian place-names:

> The azalea is grown while we sleep
> In Selinunt',
> > in Akragas
> Coke, Inst. 2.,
> > > to all cathedral churches to be
> > > read 4 times in the yeare
> > > 20. H. 3.

Like so much else in these cantos, the last line is misleading, since it suggests it was by an edict of Henry III that the Magna Charta was sent to all cathedrals and read four times a year, whereas Coke's *Institutes* make it clear that this was on the contrary an enactment of Edward I. "Selinunte" and "Akragas" (the old name of Agrigento) are ancient Greek cities in Sicily. Later in the canto (107/757-58) we come upon:

> OBIT Coke 1634 & in '49
> > > Noll cut down Charlie
> Puer Apulius . . . ver l'estate
> Voltaire could not do it;
> the french could not do it.
> > they had not Magna Charta
> in ver l'estate, Queen of Akragas
> resistent,
> > Templum aedificavit
> > Segesta

I think I know what this might mean, or what it might be *made* to mean.[1] But I can hardly care. For this is wretched writing by any standards. I said as much when *Thrones* first came out, remarking on the insanely pointless jocularity of "Noll" for Oliver Cromwell and "Charlie" for Charles I. Harsh words! But I repeated them in *Ezra Pound: Poet as Sculptor*, and nothing that has come to my notice since, including an erudite and adulatory article on these cantos by David Gordon in *Paideuma* 4 (1975), has made me want to retract my words or change my mind. Those of us who want to champion Pound do him no service at all when we try to excuse the inexcusable. And writing like this, if not indeed the writing of *Thrones* in general, I take to be inexcusable. Moreover the style faithfully mirrors the puerility of the content: to think that the barons who faced King John at Runnymede were anything like the Cokes or Hampdens who challenged the royal prerogative of the Stuarts in the seventeenth century, or that these in turn had much or anything in common with Sam and John Adams or Tom Paine, is to adopt the notorious "Whig interpretation" of English history in a sort of parody version for grade school.

At 107/759, lo and behold, yet *another* Eleanor! In fact she has made a cryptic entrance already in the fifteenth line of this canto: " . . . of Berengar his heirs was this Eleanor." This points to Eleanor *of Provence*, Edward's mother and consort of Henry III, whose reputation is as bad as that of Eleanor of Castile is good—though not for David Gordon, who seems to think that because she's said to be "of Provence," this puts her above suspicion. At any rate, this identification is now confirmed:

> & this Helianor was of the daughters, heirs
> of Raymond Berengar
> and sister of Arch. Cantaur

"Cantaur" should of course be "Cantuar," the Latin abbreviation by which the primate of England signs himself. For we read in Agnes Strickland: "The death of St. Edmund, archbishop of Canterbury, furnished Henry with a further opportunity of obliging Eleanor, by obtaining the nomination of her uncle Boniface to the primacy of England." Pound, it will be noticed, gets the kinship wrong, as well as the spelling. If there were not this evidence that at this point he is only hazily in command of what he is doing, we might ask—though to no purpose, I think—whether Eleanor's fiddling of her uncle into the see of Canterbury is presented to us for our approval, or the reverse. I don't believe Pound knows any more than we do.

And so to the last of the Sicilian references, 109/774:

> Clear deep off Taormina
> high cliff and azure beneath it
> form is cut in the lute's neck, tone is from the bowl
> Oak boughs alone over Selloi
> This wing, colour of feldspar
> phylotaxis

And doesn't this give us—faintly indeed, but unmistakably—just what we've looked for in vain in all the other Sicilian allusions: that's to say, evidence that when Pound was in Sicily he didn't go around with his eyes closed, his ears and nostrils stopped? For that surely is the disconcerting, the downright depressing, reflection that this sorry catalog must leave us with. Sicily for Pound never but once had any existence that wasn't either *verbal* (as in the wordplay on "Trinacria" or the Eleanors), or else *notional*, ideological (as providing a sort of slender mnemonic crutch for a tendentious reading of history). The contrast with Yeats is instructive, and it doesn't work in Pound's favor. The effect of the Sicilian experience on Yeats is disputed by Yeats scholars, but it is generally agreed that some effect there was. Certainly, when Yeats chaired the Irish Senate committee that commissioned the Irish coinage (so wonderfully handsome as it turned out to be), it was photographs of Sicilian Greek coins that went out to prospective designers to show them what the committee had in mind. In Pound, on the other hand . . . are we to believe that he, the long-time admirer of Pisanello, when he was in Syracuse never visited the unrivaled collection of ancient coins in the museum there? Apparently we must believe that; at least there is no evidence that, if he did visit the collection, it impinged on his consciousness. And indeed what evidence is there that Sicily as a physical presence, a quite insistent presence as generations of travelers have found it, ever modified Pound's sensibility in the least? We are not looking for additions to the canon of "sacred places." We can accept that by 1923 or 1924 the sacred places had been settled on, and there were quite enough of them. What we seek is merely evidence that Pound didn't go to Sicily with a closed mind. Pound was to mock Yeats indulgently for seeing in Notre Dame not a physical presence in worked stone, but only a symbol; yet in Sicily Pound's seems to have been the mind that was *symbologizing*.

I do not like being forced to this conclusion. It pushes back, to a disconcertingly early period in Pound's life, the first signs of that aridity, that closing of the doors of perception, which—drastically arrested and reversed though it was, at Pisa and through the first years at St. Elizabeth's—reasserted itself and wreaked the desolation of *Thrones*. Does not the use of the Na-Khi material in those cantos tell its own tale? This was material which the poet did not and could not *perceive*. Between the verbal and the notional, the perceived and perceptible were dropped out of his world. When he wrote in the last fragments

> "That I lost my center
>> fighting the world"—

this was the center that he had lost. And when he wrote "Tho' my errors and wrecks lie about me," I believe that cantos like 107 and 108 were those that he had in mind; and that he was right to judge them thus harshly.

Note

1. The meaning that might be ferreted out would identify the "it" that Voltaire and the French "could not do" with *Concord*. At any rate, that—Concord—is the best I can suggest as "Queen of Akragas," this on the admittedly dubious grounds that the temple said to be "of Concord" is the most perfect of the temples surviving at Agrigento. As for the last two lines, the fascist regime *did* reerect some fallen columns in the temple at Segesta.

TWO KINDS OF MAGNANIMITY

"Olson saved my life." Thus Pound in January 1946, in his first days at St. Elizabeth's, appealing in terror at the prospect of losing whatever sanity remained to him. How that life was saved we can now know, thanks to Catherine Seelye who has put the story together, mostly out of Olson's posthumous papers at the University of Connecticut.[1] Her tact and scrupulousness are beyond praise, and the book she has made cannot be recommended too urgently—even (perhaps especially) to those who have no special interest in, or liking for, either Charles Olson or Ezra Pound. What to do in a democratic society with the errant or aberrant citizen of genius—this question, fumbled at or glossed over by everyone who has written on Pound's case (jurists and psychiatrists, as well as biographers and critics), is here posed more

This article first appeared in the *New York Review of Books*, 1975. Reprinted with permission from *The New York Review of Books*. Copyright © 1976 Nyrev, Inc.

starkly, and explored more searchingly, than ever before. We might have guessed that Olson would do it, if any one could. . . .

And yet this probably is the first point to make. To take the force of this testimony that none of us deserves to avoid, it's not necessary to like either Olson or Pound, but it is necessary that we *respect* them. And it's not always easy to respect the author of *The Maximus Poems*, marred as they are on nearly every page by solecisms and gaucheries, by arbitrary coarsenesses in diction, punctuation, syntax, lineation. This endemic failure at the level of execution is counterbalanced, for those who are patient and sympathetic, by the audacity and grandeur of the conception. But for the moment, that's not the point—which is rather that those who have been, legitimately or at least understandably, affronted by the pretensions of Olson as poet should not therefore write him off as anything but what he was: an exceptionally earnest and magnanimous man, and a man moreover who knew, as few poets since John Milton have known, what the polity looks like from the point of view of those who administer it day by day. It's because of this— the magnanimity even more than the political expertise— that Olson's appalled and self-questioning reflections on Pound's arraignment and incarceration make all others seem puerile at best.

By "magnanimity" the last thing one means is a willingness to forgive and forget. On the contrary Olson is to be praised in the first place for the relentless hostility with which he presses the charge home:

Pound can talk all he likes about the *cultural lag* in America . . . but he's got a 200 year *political lag* in himself. It comes down to this: a rejection of the single most important human fact between Newton and the Atomic Bomb—the sudden multiple increase of the earth's population, the coming into existence of the MASSES. Pound and his kind want to ignore them. They try to lock them out. But they swarm at the windows in such numbers they black out the light and the air. And in their little place Pound and his kind suffocate, their fear turns to hate. And their hate breeds death. They want to kill. And, organized by Hitler and Mussolini, they do kill—millions. But the breeding goes on. And with it such social and political change as they shall not understand.

Pound's admirers will protest at this, but they will be wrong. If they ask for proof, let them look into their own hearts. Do they not find there (I know I do) just that suffocation Olson speaks of? Just that panicky fear, always on the verge of turning into hatred until we shamefacedly choke it back? The Masses! How can we not fear them, and fearing them, how not hate them? Olson, in several ill-written but splendidly honest verse diatribes against MUZAK, showed that he knew that fear and hatred as well as any of us. For we cannot feel what we know we *ought to* feel—that "the masses" are "just folks." (It isn't true anyway.) The fear and the incipient hatred are something that we impenitent elitists must learn to live with, not anything we can deny. For this is part of what "democracy" means, or has come to mean. And yet we haven't come to terms with that. Which is partly what Olson meant when, linking Pound with Julius Streicher, he declared:

> Our own case remains unexamined. How then shall we try men who have examined us more than we have ourselves? They know what they fight against. We do not yet know what we fight for.

That is as true now as it was in 1945, when Olson wrote it.

What Olson drives at in Pound is his fascism, not his anti-Semitism. Of the latter he gives horrific examples, which sicken him and enrage him (though as much in Mrs. Pound's genteel English version as in Pound's red-necked American). But he always treats the fascism and the anti-Semitism as two separate heads on the bill of indictment; and this I think (again I speak of myself) is what most of us stopped doing long ago. We act as if the anti-Semitism comprehended the fascism—which would be true only if all fascists were anti-Semites (they aren't), and if all anti-Semites were fascists (even less true). Hatred of Jews is something that the fascist is especially prone to, but it isn't a necessary consequence of his fascism, and in any case it's only a symptom, certainly not the root cause of his disease. (In Italian fascism it showed up only quite late, as Giorgio Bassani may remind us.) When we denounce the anti-Semitism and let the fascism take care of itself, we are fastening on what is prepolitical or sub-political, and refusing to engage ourselves on the plane of politics where, as Olson insists, we're required to vindicate our own sorts of polity against the fascist sorts. What we gain by this is obvious: our own consciences are clear, and we're no longer implicated. Or if we are implicated a little (since doubtless some Gentiles and even some Jews have anti-Jewish feelings that they're ashamed of), the implication I would guess is altogether more manageable than what happens when—Jew and Gentile alike, black as well as white—the educated elite is forced to confront its feelings about "the Masses." And Olson won't let us squirm off the hook—for him the anti-Jewishness is symptom, not cause:

> There it is. It stops you. You feel him imagining himself as the last rock of culture and civilization being swept over by

a wave of barbarism and Jews (communism and commercialism), the saviour of more than the Constitution, the saviour of all that has been culture, the snob of the West. For he is the AESTHETE, as I had Yeats speak of him. All—his pride in his memory, his sense of the internationale of writers, painters, musicians, and the aristocrats, his study of form as technique (no contours, no edges, intellectual concepts, but rounding, thrusting, as a splash of color, as Yeats described his aim in the Cantos . . .) it is all a huge AESTHETICISM, ending in hate for Jews, Reds, change, the content and matter often of disaster, a loss of future, and in that a fatality as death-full as those for whom the atom bomb is Armageddon, not Apocalypse.

Again, Pound's admirers will protest; and they will be right, insofar as Yeats's account of the *Cantos* isn't so definitive as Olson takes it to be. But the main thrust of Olson's argument is unaffected, and it can't be set aside: this great American poet (and Olson knows that Pound is all of that) was a fascist, profoundly, and no amount of talk about his affinities with Whitman will save him for democracy, nor will any attempt to treat his anti-Semitism as an unrelated pathological aberration.

Another escape hatch that Olson slams shut upon us is the device of distinguishing between Pound-the-man and Pound-the-poet. The trouble with this maneuver is that it cannot help but demote poetry. And Olson will have none of that:

Can any man, equipped to judge, find Pound other than a serious man? Can any writer honestly argue with those who shall, do, call him a crank? It's no good, that business. Around his trial you will hear it again and again. Just one of those goddamned writers. They're crazy. A Bohemian. There are writers who are such, but not Pound, despite all the vomit of his conclusions.

Pound was a serious man, and never more serious than when he was writing poetry; and his poetry drives towards just those unpalatable conclusions that Olson forces us to look in the face. If, on the other hand, from some consciousness of immaculate rectitude, we follow Allen Ginsberg in giving Pound a kiss of forgiveness—and it is in effect what David Heymann does towards the end of *The Last Rower*—it is poetry that we are presuming to forgive, not the man but "the-man-as-poet." How deep one has to go, to distinguish not "the man" from "the poet" but "the-man-who-is-the-poet," appears from Olson's splendid essay of 1949, "Granpa, Goodbye." It is impressionistic? You bet it is impressionistic, and would that we had more such "impressions":

> His power is a funny thing. There is no question he's got the jump—his wit, the speed of his language, the grab of it, the intimidation of his skillfully-wrought career. But he has little power to compel, that is, by his person. He strikes you as brittle—and terribly American, insecure. I miss weight, and an abundance. He does not seem—and this is a crazy thing to say in the face of his beautiful verse, to appear ungrateful for it—but I say it, he does not seem to have inhabited his own experience. It is almost as though he converted too fast. The impression persists, that the only life he had lived is, in fact, the literary, and, admitting its necessity to our fathers, especially to him who had such a job of clearing to do, I take it a fault. For the verbal brilliance, delightful as it is, leaves the roots dry. One has a strong feeling, coming away from him, of a lack of the amorous, down there somewhere.

> Wait. I think I've got it. Yes, Ezra *is* a tennis ball, does bounce on, off, along, over everything. But that's the outside of him. Inside it's the same, but different, he bounces, but like light bounces. Inside he is like light is, the way light behaves. In this sense he is light, light is the way of E. P.'s knowing, light is the *numen* of him, light is his way.

Maybe now I can get at this business of *amor* as of Ezra, and get at it right. It isn't a lack of the amorous, perhaps, so much as it is a completely different sense of the amorous to that which post-Christian man contains, to that which . . . the likes of Duncan, say, or myself may feel.

Of the likes of Bill W.? I am struck by the image of "fire" in "Paterson." Maybe fire is the opposite principle to light, and comes to the use of those who do not go the way of light. Fire has to consume to give off its light. But light gets its knowledge—and has its intelligence and its being—by going over things without the necessity of eating the substance of things in the process of purchasing its truth. Maybe this is the difference, the different base of not just these two poets, Bill and E. P., but something more, two contrary conceptions of love. Anyway, in the present context, it serves to characterize two different personal *via*: one achieves its clarities by way of *claritas*, the other goes about its business blind, achieves its clarities by way of what you might call *confusio*.

And this would be the point from which to look back at Olson, as Catherine Seelye wants us to, and to regard *The Maximus Poems* as embodying "the way of *confusio*." Which would raise the further question whether this way, as practiced by Olson, and by Williams in *Paterson*, isn't so unlike the ways of poetry as we have known it that to call their works "poems" doesn't merely confuse the whole issue. But that would be a strictly literary question; and it's for raising quite other questions that this book is momentous and irreplaceable.

Note

1. *Charles Olson and Ezra Pound. An Encounter at St. Elizabeths*, ed. Catherine Seelye (Grossman/Viking, 1975).

EZRA POUND AND THE ENGLISH

I have the impression that the novels of Phyllis Bottome are now little read, though I remember my mother borrowing them from the local library in Barnsley in the 1930s, and speaking of them with respect. They are too good to be forgotten, or some of them are. The one that in its day attracted most attention was *The Mortal Storm*, about the Nazis: though Phyllis Bottome herself seems to have preferred *Old Wine*, set in Vienna. The book of hers that stayed with Pound was *Private Worlds*, which he reviewed in the *New English Weekly* in 1935, and referred to twice in *Guide to Kulchur*.

Pound had known Phyllis Bottome between 1905 and 1907, when they were fellow students at the University of Pennsylvania, and it's not clear whether it is that early association, or a period later when she had caught up with him in London, that Phyllis Bottome had in mind when she wrote of how Pound tried to transform her as a writer from a talented amateur into a professional:

> I had successfully entered, at seventeen, precocious, and
> without a standard, the market of a profession which was,
> at the time I stormed it, financially profitable rather than
> intellectually exacting. Ezra provided me with a standard;
> and gingered me into an attempt to train towards it.

Certainly it is the Pound of the London years, who had profited from Ford Madox Ford's pronouncements on

---

This article first appeared in *Paideuma* 7, nos. 1 and 2 (1978). It was originally a lecture to a London conference of Pound studies in 1977.

diction, that Phyllis Bottome must have had in mind when she wrote:

> The concrete image, unruffled by an adjective, *was* a thing Ezra would willingly have died for. *Rhetoric* was a thing he would gladly have murdered; and he had already carried out his theory of honest thinking at the expense of considerable financial and perhaps emotional sacrifices. His passionate and austere sincerity acted like a torch upon the young intellectuals of his day. He cast off his home and his country because he was disgusted by its slovenliness of intellectual outlook, although he was certain (with his gifts) of success and reputation had he remained in his own land; and he was wholly unknown and unsupported when he attempted to browbeat London.

"His passionate and austere sincerity acted like a torch. . . ." This emphasis is significantly different from what it is nowadays common form to acknowledge— Pound's kindness and generosity to other writers, particularly in his London years. Behind the geniality and the ebullient showmanship, something "passionate and austere"—I know of no other testimony which strikes that necessary note so firmly. And yet this testimony is little known.

It's to be found in *From the Life* (1944): one hundred sheets of wartime austerity paper to which Phyllis Bottome commits "six studies of my friends"—that's to say, Alfred Adler, Max Beerbohm, Ivor Novello, Sara Delano Roosevelt, Ezra Pound, and Margaret MacDonald Bottome (this last the writer's American grandmother who in her forties became an influential evangelical orator). The pages on Pound are not the only ones worth reading. In particular the essay on Beerbohm is startlingly good: temperate, appreciative, sympathetic, yet in the end unsparing. And it is worth dwelling on that, to the

extent of calling into evidence another of Bottome's
books, *The Goal* (1962), p. 240:

> Ezra would have liked to see more of Max Beerbohm, whom
> he at least partially admired for his wit, although of course
> he could not have tolerated his philosophy of life. But al-
> though they lived as the only intellectual representatives of
> their own language in so small a place as Rapallo, they were
> not destined to decrease each other's mental loneliness.
>
> I found that Max Beerbohm, having once met Ezra, de-
> clined to enlarge their acquaintance. "I do not really see
> Ezra Pound in Rapallo," Max Beerbohm told me. "He seems
> out of place here. I should prefer to watch him in the pri-
> meval forests of his native land, wielding an axe against
> some giant tree. Could you not persuade him to return to a
> country in which there is so much more room?"

The consummate *silliness* of Beerbohm's sneer, quite
apart from showing just how brittle and thin was that
famous "wit" of his, has alas a representative significance
also, as we see when we put beside it Maurice Bowra,
another famous "wit," saying of Pound that he was "not
just a bore, but an *American* bore." Such frightened in-
solence about Americans is still to be found in England,
and among what the English regard as their intellectual
and artistic elite. Often enough it takes the same form as
with Beerbohm: the affectation of an anachronistic ig-
norance about what life in North America is like. And it
shows, in Beerbohm and Bowra and as it survives today,
how inevitable it was that Pound should have abandoned
England and the English just when he did. He had no al-
ternative; had he remained in London after 1920, the
antagonism to him could only have got more obdurate
and more brutal.

This is something that the Anglo-American Phyllis
Bottome, writing in England in wartime, finds it hard to
accept:

... I like to think he will be forgotten as the belligerent sycophant of Fascism and remembered as what he was when I first knew him, in the years before our little war of 1914, when he was trying to take London by storm.

Foreigners always find that a difficult process—in fact only one of them made a real success of it—and Disraeli possessed what Ezra had been denied—the elasticity and toughness of a good Jew.

Ezra had neither toughness nor elasticity: he was as rigidly intelligent as a Plymouth brother; and as vulnerable as a sea-anemone.

His unquiet personality could not outface the somnolent arrogance of the greatest city in the world.

Yet Britain needed the youthful Ezra, almost as much as Ezra needed the thickly padded hide of this favoured country ...

Or again:

... Had Jonah been less indigestible how can we be sure that the whale would have expelled him? Yet it was, I think, a tragedy for both parties that the whale of London could not keep down this nimble Jonah who distracted, but so well stimulated, her lethargic stomach. From the moment Ezra left the Anglo-Saxon world he began to suffer more and more from the isolation of his intellectual exile. This wild and wayward child of the Prophets—"a Daniel come to Judgment"—needed the thick padded hide of the antediluvian monster, whose maw he had so precipitately fled from.

One thinks rather the better of Phyllis Bottome for wanting to believe that what *had* to happen could in fact have been averted. But it should be clear to us now that the English hide which she thought so "thickly padded" was in fact morbidly sensitive—certainly as long ago as Beerbohm's spitefulness in the 1930s, and perhaps as long ago as Robert Nichols's inexcusable review of "Homage to Sextus Propertius" in 1920. If Pound had been different . . .? He would have had to be as different as T. S. Eliot; and there's an end of *that* speculation! (For Bottome herself says: "No one could write better than Ezra when he was not trying to score off T. S. Eliot by writing as badly as he knew how. . . .")

What Phyllis Bottome wants to do—what, in 1944, she *needs* to do—is to shift the blame for Pound's fascism on to something other than the heedless impetuosity of Pound himself. On the one hand she makes a speculative diagnosis of him, out of Adlerian psychology; on the other hand she half believes—but can't quite bring herself to say—that the blame lies with England, for virtually expelling him a quarter-century before. Even as she offers her diagnosis, she very touchingly envelops it in a renewed insistence on how he was still, in 1935, "passionate and austere":

Even as a young man, Ezra had always taken a determined stand on general decencies. It was not licence he wanted; alas! not even freedom—his goal was the forcible enlightenment of mankind. . . .

Even as a good Fascist Ezra found it hard to swallow the persecution of the Jews. He got away from the subject when I pounced upon it. The Teutonic mind, he said quickly, was no favourite of his: Mussolini, he implied, did not particularly dislike the Jews.

It is necessary to turn back to Ezra's childhood to find a key to that dire impatience which has led him into so strange a spiritual home as Fascist Italy. It is, alas, the spoiled and wilful child who makes whips and bloodshed take the place of wisdom and social interest!

Nevertheless in Ezra we are dealing with a creative artist who never—however impatient he was—sold his birthright for a mess of pottage. Ezra can be mistaken—more thoroughly mistaken than most people—but he has never been venal. He is one of the few people I have ever met who has never been either inflated or deflated by personal possessions. There is practically no limit to his asceticism for any purpose—other than asceticism. He lived in 1935 (when I last saw him) in the utmost simplicity, although if he had been a little more conciliatory he could always have earned enough for his comfort—and his wife's; but he never valued anything that money could buy as he valued the integrity of his sharp-shooting mind.

Elsewhere in this memoir there is more that is notable—both of documentation and diagnosis. In 1944 it took courage to write so favorably about Pound; and it may even be that Phyllis Bottome foresaw, and was trying to guard against, the peril that Pound would be in as soon as hostilities should be over. In any case, what she produced was something generous, anxious, and grateful. It should be remembered, and she should be honored for it.

I do not forget that my subject is Ezra Pound, not Max Beerbohm. Yet the circumstance of the two writers being noncommunicating neighbors in Rapallo is too piquant not to be instructive. And so I think it is worth recalling what W. H. Auden wrote of Beerbohm in 1965:

Greatly as I admire both the man and his work, I consider Max Beerbohm a dangerous influence—just how dangerous one must perhaps have been brought up in England to know. His attitude both to life and art, charming enough in him, when taken up by others as a general cultural ideal becomes something deadly, especially for the English, an intelligent but very lazy people, far too easily bored, and persuaded beyond argument that they are the *Herrenvolk*. One may be amused—though not very—that after living in Italy for forty-five years Max still could not speak Italian, but such insularity is not to be imitated. "Good sense about trivialities", he once wrote, "is better than nonsense about things that mat-

ter." True enough, but how easily this can lead to the con-
clusion that anyone who attempts to deal with things that
matter must be a bore, that rather than run the risk of talk-
ing nonsense one should play it safe and stick to charming
trifles. . . .

This, remember, is W. H. Auden, whom for many years
some people in England have regarded as himself too
anxious not to bore, too anxious always to amuse. If
this suggests that there are other sorts of English people
than the sort Auden has in his sights, on the other hand
it lends point and force to his censure of Beerbohm, and
of what Beerbohm stands for in English life. Auden goes
on:

> As it is, he slyly suggests that minor artists may look down
> their noses at major ones and that "important" work may
> be left to persons of an inferior kennel, like the Russians,
> the Germans, the Americans, who, poor dears, know no
> better. The great cultural danger for the English is, to my
> mind, their tendency to judge the arts by the values appro-
> priate to the conduct of family life. Among brothers and
> sisters it is becoming to entertain each other with witty re-
> marks, hoaxes, family games and jokes, unbecoming to be
> solemn, to monopolize the conversation, to talk shop, to
> create emotional scenes. But no art, major or minor, can be
> governed by the rules of social amenity. The English have a
> greater talent than any other people for creating an agree-
> able family life; that is why it is such a threat to their artistic
> and intellectual life. If the atmosphere were not so charm-
> ing, it would be less of a temptation. In postwar Britain,
> the clothes, accents, and diction of the siblings may have
> changed, but, so far as I can judge, the suffocating insular
> coziness is just the same.

Here, as often with the author of *Thankyou, Fog,* we
may well suspect that Auden generalizes about English
life too much on the basis of his own late-Edwardian

childhood in a comfortable rentier household. And yet I wouldn't dismiss out of hand Auden's claim that what he says of our family life holds as true of Coronation Street as of Lowndes Square. In any case, enveloped though it is in ingratiating compliments to us on how charming we are in the bosoms of our families, the indictment is quite firm and it is unsparing: "suffocating insular coziness." Most of all worth remembering is the trenchant declaration: ". . . no art, major or minor, can be governed by the rules of social amenity." It was because Pound behaved always in the spirit of this remark that he could not fail to offend Englishmen of the type of Beerbohm and Bowra, and that he continues to offend their likes and their successors (in all social classes) at the present day, as, for instance, his confrere T. S. Eliot did not and does not. On this issue indeed the comparison with Eliot is inescapable. Eliot very early learned and bowed to the English rule that social amenity must not be disturbed—alike in his life-style and, after *Poems 1920*, in his poetic style also, he observed this rule punctiliously. Pound saw him doing it, and chuckled indulgently; it was what he meant by dubbing Eliot "the Possum" (opossum, the creature that escapes danger by shamming dead). And when we remember what Eliot did with the gibe, taking it over in the title of *Old Possum's Book of Favourite Cats*, that collection of whimsical fireside charades in verse, we may well think again about Auden's comment that in English family life "it is becoming to entertain each other with witty remarks, hoaxes, family games and jokes." Is it perhaps true that for many of the English, poetry has never been anything else but a superior parlor game? We might begin to think so if we reflected that in parlor games the rules never change, and then noticed that this year the most accomplished of our poets in their forties published, sixty years after Pound's *Lustra* and Eliot's *Prufrock*, an ambitious poem in the shape of fifteen interlinked pentameter sonnets.

However, a safer and a wiser idea is to take up what I began with: Phyllis Bottome telling how Pound, when they were both young, tried to turn her as a writer from an amateur into a professional. It was, of course, what he tried to do with everyone that he thought worth the trouble. And once again it was this unrelenting professionalism in Pound that set, and continues to set, Englishmen's teeth on edge. For in our national tradition, in the arts as until recently in sports, it is the amateur who is most admired; and Auden's charming joker by the Christmas hearth is only a particular version of the amateur. He observes the prohibition against "talking shop," whereas Pound through his London years seems never to have talked anything else. (Once again Eliot knew, or soon learned, better.) And the most Anglophobe of Pound's books is, appropriately, the one that is most full of shoptalk—though of shoptalk of a special kind, the talk of the master to his apprentices in the shop that is a workshop, the *atelier* where the talk that goes on is the vehicle by which an artistic tradition is transmitted, not in conceptualizing, and tendentious readings of history, but where it is *concrete,* in tricks of the trade and rules of thumb and words to the wise. I have in mind *How To Read,* a disastrously misnamed little treatise, since its real subject is How to Write, and it is addressed to what Pound called (with the engagingly dated Edwardian elegance that he never wholly shed) "the neophyte"—that is to say, to the young American writer who wants to know as soon as possible, though at the expense of considerable exertion which he is prepared for, how to assemble his kit of tools for the job in hand and others that he can dimly foresee. When Pound revised and expanded this to make

The ABC of Reading (the title is *still* a misnomer), he winkled out of it most of the anti-Englishness that had been present in the first version, when Pound was still smarting from what he took to be England's rejection of him eight years before, in 1920. I have argued elsewhere that Pound was prepared to take instruction, as well as to give it; that when he first came to London in 1908, he was looking for masters to whom he might apprentice himself; that he found them in the Irishman W. B. Yeats and the maverick Englishman Ford Madox Ford (whose professionalism about writing still denies him in England the recognition that he gets abroad); and (so I have speculated, though I know it cannot be proved) that Pound sought the same relationship with another Englishman, Laurence Binyon, who was too cagey to go along with the idea. Before we leave this topic, with some doubtless well-received witticisms about the American *ateliers* that are called Schools of Creative Writing, let us ask ourselves how an artistic tradition *is* transmitted from generation to generation in England, if it is not transmitted in the way that Pound took for granted. And let me assist such reflections by reporting that a gifted and earnest English poet of thirty-two, whom I met this very summer, not only confessed that he had never read through Basil Bunting's *Briggflatts*, but quite plainly saw no reason why he ever should.

We can stage a little comedy for ourselves if we pick out two expressions that I used in my last paragraph, and imagine ourselves presenting them to the startled and unwelcoming gaze of Max Beerbohm. They are the expressions "kit of tools" and "job in hand." We may doubt that Beerbohm had the acumen or the catholicity to respond to this provocation as conclusively as he should. But in that case, let us do it for him. The conclusive objection to "kit of tools" or "job in hand" as appropriate expressions when we talk of poetry, is in some late lines by Eliot:

> Because one has only learnt to get the better of words
> For the thing one no longer has to say, or the way in which
> One is no longer disposed to say it.

It is the occasion which determines what figurations of language are appropriate to it, and no one poetic occasion duplicates any other. To this extent and in this way the English distrust of the professional writer can and must be vindicated. It was what Pound found out the hard way, when the recurrent occasions of *The Cantos* compelled him time and again, not infrequently, to go against the precepts that he had promulgated himself when he was the fugleman for imagism and vorticism— for instance (and it *is* only the most obvious instance), the prohibition against archaic diction. What's more, though it seems not to be generally realized, Pound recognized what had happened and acknowledged it; he did so in the public welcome he gave to Binyon's translations of Dante, which employ a very archaic and convoluted diction indeed. And this was not the only occasion on which he protested, in the 1920s and 1930s, at having the precepts that were formulated to meet the special conditions of 1914 taken as absolute and binding for all poetic situations at all times. He does not, however, retract his proposal that the precepts of the imagist manifesto *are* still the best rules of thumb for "the neophyte," the beginner in his 'prentice-work; and for what it is worth my own experience in the workshop certainly bears that out. The notion that we crucially need, I think, to do justice to the conflicting claims of the amateur and the professional in these matters, is the idea of *thresholds*. In verse writing, as in virtually any other human activity we may think of, there are thresholds to be reached and crossed: below a certain threshold of practice and expertise, the attitude of the amateur produces only work that is "amateurish" (and heaven knows, we see plenty of that all around us); above a certain threshold of facility, the attitude of the professional produces work that is glib, facile, heartless, and academic—and we see plenty of that, too. Though I think neither Eliot nor Pound explicitly used the idea of "the threshold," the idea is surely implicit in the criticism of both men; and it is an implication that in our own criticism, and our own practice as verse writers, is almost universally ignored.

At any rate, in this way if in no other, the English ideal of the artist as amateur has a continuing validity— and one that it behoves us, as Poundians, to acknowledge more often than we do. It is an idea—the idea that the practice of our art should *ideally* be an avocation rather than a vocation—which has a distinguished and ancient lineage, to be traced back through the English bourgeois idea of "the gentleman" to the Italian aristocratic idea of "the courtier." Yeats's poem, "In Memory of Major Robert Gregory," is centrally concerned with this, as when he associates Robert Gregory with that paradigm of the English courtier, Philip Sidney. And during the years when Pound was most under Yeats's influence, Pound too embraced this ideal—as when in 1912 he went with Yeats and some others to pay an act of homage to one of the last English representatives of the type, the Sussex squire Wilfred Scawen Blunt:

> But to have done instead of not doing
>   this is not vanity
> To have, with decency, knocked
> That a Blunt should open
>   To have gathered from the air a live tradition

or from a fine old eye the unconquered flame
This is not vanity.
    Here error is all in the not done,
all in the diffidence that faltered.

However, we know from Yeats's letters even more than his poems that he thought the last possibility for aristocratic ease in the arts had disappeared when Robert Gregory was shot down over France in 1915. And I think it could be maintained that when Pound left England in 1920, it testified to a similar recognition by him that the amateur ideal in the arts, however admirable in the abstract, and however rich its achievements under earlier structures of society, under the conditions of mass democracy could mean only amateurishness in technique, and thin-skinned insolence in debate. Who is to say that Yeats and Pound were wrong? Not I, certainly.

What is important to realize is that for Yeats certainly, and I think at times for Pound also, the only alternative open was a sorry second best. Yeats in a letter specifically invoked the name of Wilfred Scawen Blunt on one of many occasions when he girded in rage against the "unnatural labour" that verse writing had become for him, with the disappearance of the less egalitarian society that Gregory and Blunt stood for. Professionalism in writing was what Yeats resentfully found himself condemned to; but he didn't like it, and he never pretended to. Obviously, the same cannot be said of Pound. On the contrary, as I have insisted, one indelibly American thing about Pound from the day when he first reached London was his, as it must seem to us, excessive faith in knowhow, in a communicable "bag of tricks." And yet there is his tribute, as late as the Pisan years, to Blunt; there is the fact that his friendship with Yeats did not end except with Yeats's death; and there is above all the fact that his disenchantment with mass democracy kept pace with Yeats's, and culminated for him as for Yeats in the false alternative of fascism. I believe a close examination of his recorded opinions, and of the idiom in which those opinions were expressed (an idiom, even to the end, as much British as American), would show that Pound too was not insensible to the ideal of the aristocratic amateur in the arts, and was at least sometimes resentful, just as Yeats was, that political and socioeconomic developments had made that attitude to the arts impracticable and sterile. If so, we English Poundians, even as we castigate our countrymen for clinging to the norm of the amateur in an age when that norm is unserviceable, may well spare more than just wistful nostalgia for this ideal that survives among us only in a debased and anachronistic version.

One reason for insisting on this possibility is to prevent us from being too complacent and self-congratulating about what we are engaged in, here and now. We should beware of supposing that, if Pound from the shades is looking at this present occasion, he is unreservedly gratified by what he sees. Weekend conference and seminar and study group, doctoral dissertations, and communally compiled working papers toward another *Annotated Index*—we may agree, as I do, that in present historical conditions these are the best or the only ways of responding to the achievement of a very great, though of course imperfect, poet. We may even feel, as certainly I do, that some of the later cantos are of such a nature that it's hard to conceive in *any* age of a way of encountering them other than the way we're here embarked upon. And yet we need to remember—Pound, I think, would have wanted us to remember—what a late-come development this is in the relations between a poet and his readers, how recent this is, and, in the perspective of history, how bizarre. We may surely placate the shade of Max Beerbohm sufficiently to acknowledge that the danger we run in approaching poetry this way is indeed the danger of one sort of professionalism—specialized and therefore blinkered, inflexible, and humorless. I suspect that Pound is rueful at best when he looks down and sees us industriously annotating out of Sir Edward Coke canto 107, without noticing that the English language is in that canto handled with none of the sensitivity that would make those labors worthwhile.

What I am saying is that a lot of the common English objections to Ezra Pound have substance, and would be worth taking seriously, if only we could be sure that they were advanced in good faith, in humility, and with compassion. Unfortunately the tone in which they are expressed, and the language they are couched in, prevent our taking them in that way, and recall for us rather the heads of Auden's indictment: "lazy . . . too easily bored . . . persuaded beyond argument . . ." Accordingly, an assembly such as this in England—and let me remind you there have been earlier ones, at Sheffield and Keele— is an act of homage to a great and greatly maligned poet; but it is also, and cannot help but be, a patriotic demonstration against "suffocating insular coziness."

A Fascist Poem

Yeats's "Blood and the Moon"

There have been so many commentaries on Yeats's po-
etry that no one—certainly not I—can claim to be con-
versant with all or even most of them. However, to the
best of my knowledge, no one has yet read out of Yeats's
"Blood and the Moon" the dismaying and alarming
meaning that I find it presents to me. The poem first ap-
peared in spring 1928, in Pound's Paris magazine, *The
Exile*; and this may be to the point, for I read the poem
as expressing a fascism more thorough-going than Pound
would have professed at that time, and in some ways more
unpalatable than Pound would profess at *any* time. This
is not in the least to extenuate Pound's fascism, but it *is*
meant to suggest how much more indulgent we have been,
and continue to be, towards Yeats's fascism than towards
Pound's. When we are compelled—for instance, by Conor
Cruise-O'Brien—to recognize that in old age Yeats was
quite consciously and voluntarily a fascist, we still try to
huddle this aberration away into his very last collection,
as we find it for instance in the unmistakable allusions
to racism and eugenics in "Under Ben Bulben," the poem
of 1938 that stands last in the *Collected Poems*, declaring:

> Know that when all words are said
> And a man is fighting mad,
> Something drops from eyes long blind,
> He completes his partial mind . . .

The point of looking at "Blood and the Moon," un-
doubtedly a less impressive poem than "Under Ben
Bulben," is to establish, if I am right, that Yeats was no
less a fascist a good ten years earlier.

Since "Blood and the Moon" is not a very well-known
poem, I must be allowed to quote it in full:

I.

Blessed be this place,
More blessed still this tower;
A bloody, arrogant power
Rose out of the race
Uttering, mastering it,
Rose like these walls from these
Storm-beaten cottages—
In mockery I have set
A powerful emblem up,
And sing it rhyme upon rhyme
In mockery of a time
Half dead at the top.

II.

Alexandria's was a beacon tower, and Babylon's
An image of the moving heavens, a log-book
   of the sun's journey and the moon's;
And Shelley had his towers, thought's crowned
   powers he called them once.

I declare this tower is my symbol; I declare
This winding, gyring, spiring treadmill
   of a stair is my ancestral stair;
That Goldsmith and the Dean, Berkeley and Burke
   have travelled there.

Swift beating on his breast in sibylline frenzy blind
Because the heart in his blood-sodden breast
   had dragged him down into mankind,
Goldsmith deliberately sipping at the honey-pot of his mind.

And haughtier-headed Burke that proved the State a tree,
That this unconquerable labyrinth of the birds,
   century after century,
Cast but dead leaves to mathematical equality;

And God-appointed Berkeley that proved all things a dream,
That this pragmatical, preposterous pig of a world,
   its farrow that so solid seem,
Must vanish on the instant if the mind but change its theme;

Saeva Indignatio and the labourer's hire,
The strength that gives our blood and state
   magnanimity of its own desire;
Everything that is not God consumed with intellectual fire.

III.

The purity of the unclouded moon
Has flung its arrowy shaft upon the floor.
Seven centuries have passed and it is pure,
The blood of innocence has left no stain.
There, on blood-saturated ground, have stood
Soldier, assassin, executioner,
Whether for daily pittance or in blind fear
Or out of abstract hatred, and shed blood,
But could not cast a single jet thereon.
Odour of blood on the ancestral stair!
And we that have shed none must gather there
And clamour in drunken frenzy for the moon.

IV.

Upon the dusty, glittering windows cling,
And seem to cling upon the moonlit skies,
Tortoiseshell butterflies, peacock butterflies,
A couple of night-moths are on the wing.
Is every modern nation like the tower,
Half dead at the top? No matter what I said,
For wisdom is the property of the dead,
A something incompatible with life; and power,
Like everything that has the stain of blood,

A property of the living; but no stain
Can come upon the visage of the moon
When it has looked in glory from a cloud.

It is awkward to have to start accounting for this poem
by bringing in information from outside it, but it will
save time to do so. Accordingly, I start with what Joseph
Hone says about it in his pioneering biography (*W. B.
Yeats 1865-1939*, 1942), where we learn that this is one
of two poems written under the immediate impact of
the assassination of Kevin O'Higgins, Ireland's authori-
tarian "strong man," whom Yeats knew well and admired,
shot down on a Sunday morning in July 1927. Particu-
larly pertinent is Hone's quoting from *On the Boiler*, the
last piece of prose that Yeats wrote, where (I quote
Hone) "he was to place O'Higgins in his Irish 'saga' with
Berkeley, Swift, Burke, Grattan, Synge, Lady Gregory."
This is important because it suggests that the litany of
names in the second section of the poem is only acci-
dentally Anglo-Irish and Protestant; it is meant to be
Irish, and the addition of O'Higgins makes it so. Yeats,
when he added that name in *On the Boiler*, made the
point explicitly: "If the Catholic names are few on the
list, history will soon fill the gap. . . ."

History *will.* . . . The future tense gives another clue:
the litany of names in the poem is not backward-looking,
elegiac, but forward-looking and menacing. And indeed
the poem itself virtually says as much:

A bloody, arrogant power
Rose out of the race . . .

As an account of Ireland's recorded past this is just un-
true, as Yeats's Irish readers would be the first to realize.
The bloody power did not rise out of the Irish race, but
was imposed upon it—time and again, from the days of

the Anglo-Norman overlordship that left behind the tower Thoor Ballylee in which and about which Yeats is writing. Thus, he is writing of an Ascendancy that *will* come; the Ascendancy that has been is a sort of guide to this, but with the difference (less crucial to Yeats than to many) that the new Ascendancy will rise out of the race—naturally, so a fascist would say—whereas the Ascendancy that has been was imposed by a colonizing power on the race subjugated and colonized. It is natural, when we first encounter the roll call of Goldsmith and Swift, Berkeley and Burke, to suppose that it serves the same purpose as when a similar roll is called in other poems and in a famous Senate speech; that is to say, to stand for the minority, once ascendant but now dispossessed, for which Yeats in the Republic is making himself a spokesman. But this is a blind, a false scent deliberately laid by Yeats who, in 1928, as Cruise-O'Brien explains, chose not to express his fascist sentiments openly. The charge of "fascism" has yet to be substantiated, as I am aware; but at least we must realize that in this poem more is going on than meets the eye.

"Uttering, mastering it"—the avowed mockery with which this "powerful emblem" is set up derives from the difference between "uttering" and "mastering." To utter and articulate the race consciousness is certainly in one sense to master the race. In fact it may be the most perdurable sort of mastery. But it differs from other sorts of mastery in that it is achieved without the spilling of blood; those who achieve the sort of mastery that is utterance (and they include all the names in the second section of the poem) are shut out from the blood tie that, in the third section, binds together master and mastered, the assassin and his victim, the leader and his henchmen, the native Irish, the Norman-Irish, and the Anglo-Irish. This is the point of bringing in the figures of Percy Bysshe Shelley and the Alexandrian and

Babylonian astronomers. Some commentators—for instance, Denis Donoghue in a volume called *An Honoured Guest*—can see in these allusions nothing but a muddling distraction. But they are crucial, because they show that the Anglo-Irish names which follow are introduced not just as Anglo-Irish (which we have suspected already), but also not as *Irish*—they are the names of utterers, articulators, in a word *intellectuals*. "His towers, thought's crowned powers," in relation to Shelley, is a jawbreaking, uncouth expression, but what it says is important. The tower is Yeats's "ancestral stair," partly because it is Irish, but far more because Yeats is an intellectual. Yeats is of the Ascendancy to come only in being the self-appointed laureate and apologist of that Ascendancy that will be, as Burke and the rest were apologists for the Ascendancy that once was.

Thus, in the third section ("we that have shed none"), the "we" is not modern man as against men of the past. The "we" is Yeats *and* Shelley *and* Burke *and* Berkeley *and* Goldsmith. And all of them are in drunken frenzy because they all want the blood bond which they are debarred from through being articulators, apologists, utterers. This means, so the poem says, that the assassins and their victims are "innocent" in a way the articulators never can be. And it is surely here—in the grotesque inversion by which "innocence" is reserved for those who spill each other's blood—that the charge of "fascism" can be made to stick. Yeats is a great poet, and we can respect the honesty of the logic that led him to this point; but what he says is sick and loathsome:

> Odour of blood on the ancestral stair!
> And we that have shed none must gather there
> And clamour in drunken frenzy for the moon.

Moreover, the attempt to "shoot the moon" is doomed to failure; even though the purity of a lunar monument like Berkeley's philosophy is never tarnished, yet even for Berkeley the end is in frustration, since power is humanly attainable whereas wisdom isn't—if only because the dead, who are truly wise, can never communicate their wisdom. (The commentators tell us, no doubt correctly, that the butterflies are, as in Dante, disembodied spirits too fragile to break into the lighted tower of human contemplation through the window to which they flutter. What it is beneath a commentator's dignity to say is that they are also, doubtless, the night moths which the elderly poet saw outside the windowpane when he raised his eyes from the page he was working on.)

Thus every modern nation is—like the tower of Thoor Ballylee, with its concrete roof and unrepaired top story— "half dead at the top," not just because in nonfascist states the elite is not self-chosen, and thus not "natural"; but also because, even in the fascist state to be hoped for, the clerisy, the apologists for the regime, will be excluded from the blood tie, disabled by guilt at this exclusion, and by frustration at knowing that their objective (the moon—they are lunatics) is unattainable.

Certain reflections present themselves. For it would surely be quite wrong to leave the impression that "Blood and the Moon" has merely *diagnostic* significance, as showing the sociopolitical aberrations that one great poet, or even a generation of poets, could fall into. On the contrary, this poem, that seems at first sight so intensely, even parochially, Irish in its terms of reference, turns out when we look at it to be passing judgment on matters that are not peculiarly Irish at all. We may note in the first place that on our reading of the poem the poet is given no specially privileged status. He, and the artist generally, is downgraded, radically—Goldsmith, for instance, is presented as a mere epicure of the intellect, and the one poetic icon that is set up in the poem (the tower) is ravaged with mockery that is self-mockery; the writers in the poem are seen in their capacity as intellectuals, members of a clerisy, not as image makers. Does this mean that fascism has no role for the image maker to play? However that may be, it is not for nothing that I have used the Coleridgean term, "clerisy." Let us call it "intelligentsia," if we find that more fashionable term more comfortable. Certainly what the poem is concerned with is the function of "the intellectuals," considered as a distinct and in some degree corporate body in the modern state. And from that point of view the poem surely is an extreme formulation of the anguish felt by the intellectual under the repressive tolerance (as we used to call it some years ago) which is wished upon him by modern societies such as the British and the American. In Yeats's writing early and late this is a constant theme—the wish of the writer to be *held responsible*, to be *called to account for* the consequences of his own utterances:

> Did that play of mine send out
> Certain men the English shot?

Yeats wants the answer, yes! And if certain penalties attend upon the answer "yes," he wants, quite desperately, to undergo those penalties. The supposedly enlightened toleration which permits a writer to say what he pleases, on the supposition that he will never be brought to book for the consequences, is what every writer must be glad of in his private and domestic capacity, at the same time as he indignantly deplores it, in his capacity as a member of the same international elite that includes, or once included, Boris Pasternak and Osip Mandelstam. The writer who believes in the nobility and necessity of his calling may even be pushed to the extreme and paradoxical position of yearning for those regimes, fascist or communist, in which his activity is thought important and influential enough to be worth persecuting and proscribing.

John Peck's *Shagbark*

In the copy he has sent to me, John Peck has written:

> To Donald Davie,
> master stone-carver,
> this tree-rind.

Let the handsome compliment be deserved or not, the terms of it certainly clarify, for such a reader as me, the contract which this civil but exacting poet offers us. We are invited to a vegetarian banquet: the images which are central to this poetry, which carry the burden of its most intimate meanings, are insistently vegetable. Grasses and underbrush and trees—time and again, trees—are the defining presences of a world that is not the less menacing for being, quite luxuriantly, arboreal and floral.

This is deliberate, and deliberately challenging. For me the deliberation shows up nowhere so clearly as in a poem called "The Upper Trace," which opens the second of four sections in a collection which (one comes to recognize) is assembled with as much calculation as is each of the poems thus assembled, and each line within each

This article first appeared in *Shenandoah* 24, no. 1 (Fall 1972). Copyright 1972 by Washington and Lee University, reprinted from *Shendoah: The Washington and Lee University Review*, with the permission of the Editor.

poem. "The Upper Trace" takes us into a landscape of stone, above the timberline; into it and through it, as high as the glaciers, where stone—emblem of the immobile and enduring—is seen to be conditioned, if not indeed commanded, by what is on the contrary infinitely mobile and fluid, the element of water frozen and thawing and again frozen:

> What is it throws the light back
> In steady points from the valley?
> He said, that is the sheer face
> Of granite sliced and smoothed by this,
> The tributary ice.
> A horse strange to this country
> Will smell the polished stone
> And test it with his hoof,
> Thinking it water.

The "he" in this poem cannot be identified; and this indeed is the rule with the "he" and the "you" in Peck's poems generally. However, this poem is inscribed "for Y. W."—who surely cannot be other than Yvor Winters. And though Winters has poems which acknowledge and even celebrate the fundamental process of reality as bewildering metamorphosis, yet we think of him as on the whole a poet of stone or of the lapidary effect, one who speaks of the poetic subject, the poetic "matter," as something other than the poet and confronting him; whereas in the world of *Shagbark*, as for instance in the world of Stevens, the traffic between subject and object is always too various and glancing for "confrontation" to be the word for it. In particular, poem after poem by Winters enacts a drama in which the precarious solidity of stony land is threatened and undermined by ocean, destructively fluid; and in a poem by Peck called "Involuntary Portrait" the same antithesis is set up and worked out—so that one may legitimately see Winters or someone in this respect very like him, in the figure who (we are told) has written:

> In time's teeth, as the unbaffled can,
>
> Yes, countermarched whole seasons in your war—
> Made spite and justice somehow both your friends.
> All this I have admired, and more—
>
> Yet, when you ask me to approve,
> To foresee victory, I see instead
> Your figure strangely set at great remove
>
> Against a headland, posing there . . .

The poem ends:

> Below and always,
> The slope-heaved billows stupidly explode.

And the surprisingly fierce word, "stupidly," is one instance of many in this collection which exemplify a distinction not purely of style, but moral and humane. For if this is a poet who is firmly persuaded that the vegetable metaphor tells more truly than the lapidary does, he takes small comfort from that; he comes to the conviction reluctantly, even grudgingly. Almost, it seems, he wishes that the lapidaries were in the right of it. Consistency, steadfastness—these qualities the moralist in him applauds, even as the artist in him sees them dissolve into pathos.

There is a similar moment at the end of what is perhaps the most elaborate and ambitious poem in the whole book, "Cider and Vesalius," which I predict will become a very famous poem indeed. Here the vegetable truth of cider ("Like a fruit wine with earth/Clouding its sweetness") finally takes precedence of the analytical truth of the heroic anatomist, Vesalius. But this is how it does so, in the last lines of the poem:

> This glass drying to stains
> Of cider, while the autumn
> Milkweed lifts into air,
> Silk wrinkling in wind,
> White inchworms draped from trees
> At loose in the loose wind,
> Fouling whatever moves,
> Squandering transformation.

This image chimes with another earlier in the poem—of the rags of malefactor's flesh fluttering from the gibbet from which the young Vesalius filches piecemeal the material he needs for his anatomical studies. The vegetable world of squandered transformations does not, in Peck's vision, override or bypass the world of Good and Evil, as it sometimes seems to do for Stevens. On the contrary it compels us to acts of moral choice at every turn, even as it complicates those choices. And of course this is traditional. For the act of Original Sin was the plucking and eating of fruit from a tree, as Peck reminds us in a poem called "Apple," which as I read it could not have been more orthodox if it had been written by Edwin Muir, though it has a sardonic power that Muir could command only at his best.

It is very seldom that one can take stock of a first book of poems by proceeding at once to its meaning, to the vision which it articulates. Usually one has to talk of "promise," of a repertoire of stylistic resources not all of which are as yet at the young poet's command, of where and how he must extend his range if he is to progress, of directions that will be dangerous for him as well as others that will be profitable. With Peck this would be impertinent. His several styles are all firmly under control, and he switches from one to another with unflustered tact and decorum and according to no predetermined alignment of himself with this or that "school." The sensuous fullness of his presentations is what strikes first, perhaps, and the sinewy opulence of his writing accordingly recalls a kind of writing that was more often met with twenty-five years ago (I think of the best poems of Léonie Adams) than it is today when a sort of neo-Rousseauism has done so much damage to American writing. But this is to say only that here once again we have a poet addressing himself humbly and yet with assurance to honoring and extending the *whole* of the tradition he is heir to (Whitman as much as Frost, Pound as much as Stevens), and not to some idiosyncratically or perversely preferred strand within it.

American Literature
The Canon

I come before you asking what I hope are patient questions, as pretty much an ignoramus, certainly an amateur. This has not much to do with my being a subject of Her Majesty Queen Elizabeth II, but it has something to do with that. And I should like to begin by spending a few minutes on the rather peculiar difficulties that a British reader feels when he approaches American literature. These difficulties will not be unfamiliar to you because they are a mirror image of what you as Americans encounter when you consider modern British literature. You know that modern British literature is a foreign literature to you, and yet quite plainly it is not foreign in the same way as French literature is, or Italian, or German, or Spanish. And the Englishman regards American literature in the same way: it is somehow a foreign literature, and yet it isn't, it is not foreign in the way other literatures are. As a matter of fact, of course, there are people on both sides of the Atlantic (though they are more prominent and numerous in the United Kingdom than in the United States), who would deny even this much, who would deny that the other English-speaking literature is a foreign literature at all. This is an attitude which

This was originally a lecture delivered at the University of Montana.

was very common, particularly among the English, up to a couple of generations ago, and the people who still hold this view in England are, for the most part, in their declining years. They would say that "English literature" is a term applied to literature in English wherever it is written, whether in North America, in Australasia, Polynesia, Asia, emergent Africa, anywhere. And in fact, there are quite strong arguments which can be brought to support this nowadays very unfashionable, and I think dying, attitude. In particular, people of this way of thinking can ask: If I as an English reader am to regard the literature of the United States as a foreign literature, am I not to regard the literature of Australia as foreign likewise? Indeed, am I not as an Englishman to regard Scottish literature written in English as a foreign literature, Anglo-Irish literature as foreign, Anglo-Welsh literature as foreign? These are difficult and ticklish questions to answer because what is involved in them is a sense of national identity on the part of various peoples. If we are to say that the literature of the United States exists as a literature foreign to English, but we refuse to recognize, let us say, New Zealand literature as having the same sort of status, patriotic New Zealanders are likely to be annoyed, for it seems we are denying to New Zealand a cultural independence and identity which we are allowing to the United States. Particularly, here in the state of Montana, how can we fail to reflect upon the vast nation to the north of us? Is Canadian literature an independent literature foreign both to the British Isles and to the United States, or is it not? Is Canadian culture still in a colonial and dependent relation, and if it is, which nation is it culturally a colonial dependency of? Of the United Kingdom, or of the United States?

If I have any Canadians in this audience, they are undoubtedly feeling already outraged and affronted. What's certain is that the very phrase, "American literature," as enshrined in our curricula, is anything but helpful, for one thing we have to say of such "American literature" is that it isn't the literature of America. The literature of America is written in Spanish, Portuguese, French, Quechua, Nahuatl, and various other Indian languages, as well as in English. Even if we take American literature to mean the literature of *North* America, we still, if we are to be logical, must recognize that much of that literature is written in languages other than English, since much Canadian literature, for instance, is in French. British and American alike, we stand convicted, I fear, of overweening presumption in supposing that literature in English is for most practical purposes shared between the United Kingdom and the United States. Of course this is not true. On the contrary, one of the most remarkable things about the language which we speak and write in common is that it is more likely than any other language to become a *world* language. A great number of the most significant and beautiful poems and stories and plays of newly independent Africa are in fact written in our language, and we pay all too little attention to that fact. If we paid more attention to such facts, our imperialistic presumptions, American and British alike, would be cut down to size in a way which would be very salutary for both nations. The old and now discredited idea that English literature was literature written in English wherever written, and hence that American literature as an independent and autonomous phenomenon did not and could not exist, had at least this to recommend it: that it took account, as *we* find it very difficult to do, of the literature in the English language that is being produced in regions of the world quite remote both from the United Kingdom and from the United States.

However, it is clear that that old view has been discredited and cannot long survive among us, whether in the British Isles or the United States. It smacks too much of the presumptuousness of the metropolitan culture centered upon London, regarding all the other English-speaking cultures as colonial dependencies. And I think there are stronger arguments against it. For we cannot believe that literature exists, or is produced, in a "pure" realm, quite unaffected by the political and social and physical dimensions of the region where it is produced and responded to. Accordingly, the sheerly physical, geographical scale of regions of the world like Canada, the United States, and Australia, so different from the small-scale physical landscape of the British Isles, is enough in my view to ensure that the English-language literature produced in those regions either is now, or in due course will be, autonomous and independent of British literature. Accordingly, I have no difficulty in conceding that the literature of the United States is, from my point of view as a British reader, a foreign literature (in some sense).

But the question now presents itself: At what stage did the literature of the United States *become* a literature foreign to the Englishman? And when I consult authorities, I find a bewildering variety of answers to this crucial question. At one extreme I find people claiming that the devotional poet Edward Taylor (1642?-1729), who wrote his poems as a Calvinist minister in New England, is already an ornament of an American literature conceived of as distinct from British—this despite the fact that Taylor spent his first twenty-five years in his native England! At the other extreme, I find William Carlos Williams in our own time still castigating his contemporaries, Eliot and Ezra Pound, for having lived abroad and having seemed to conceive of themselves as contributing to a European or a world culture, thus delaying the achievement of genuine independence and autonomy for the literature of the United States. In between these extremes is to be found the figure of Ralph Waldo Emerson, asserting that in the middle of the nineteenth century the United States had still not achieved a cultural independence from Britain to match the political independence which had been claimed in 1776 and won by 1783. Emerson exhorted his fellow Americans to achieve that cultural independence, and he saluted that one of his fellow Americans who, in his view, had achieved this for himself and for his countrymen—that is to say, Walt Whitman. Groping for guidance in the fog of my imperfect knowledge, I find this attitude of Emerson's the most plausible on offer. Nevertheless, it does not solve all my problems, for if Walt Whitman had indeed liberated the American writer from dependence upon British models and precedents, there were plenty of American writers in the next two generations who did not realize they had been liberated, who did not thank Whitman for the release he had brought them. Well into the present century there appear to have been American writers who still looked for ultimate approval to London rather than Boston or New York, who were to this extent psychologically still "colonials." Moreover, in those generations after Whitman, there are the two massive figures of Henry James and T. S. Eliot, American by birth but British by adoption. Am I to regard Henry James's *Portrait of a Lady* and T. S. Eliot's *Four Quartets* as works belonging to a literature foreign to me as an Englishman? At this point it may well be felt that the whole discussion is getting silly; it cannot be right for these intriguing and important questions of national tradition in literature to be reduced to the accident of what sort of passport a given writer flashes at the international frontier. You will see, however, that I have already arrived at what I advertised as the principal concern of this talk; that is to say, which writers belong in American literature, and which others don't. Is Henry James yours, or mine? Is T. S. Eliot mine, or yours? Is W. H. Auden mine until 1939, yours after 1940? And does it matter?

As it happens, however, I am less interested in the twentieth-century writers as to whom this question can be raised, than I am in certain writers of the seventeenth and eighteenth centuries. I had the experience not long ago in a graduate seminar of having an American student protest that for her Chaucer, Shakespeare, and Milton were foreign authors. She contended that she ought to be able to study her own literature, American, without have to "carry" some English also. I responded by saying that these great writers were as much hers as mine, since they were great writers in the English language at a time when the two branches of the English-speaking people on either side of the Atlantic had not yet split apart into two distinct national identities. As it happens, though, the student who made this comment was black, and I could not fail to realize that if indeed her ancestors were already in the continental United States at the time when the Declaration of Independence was signed, they were here through no choice of their own, and in a disfranchised, deliberately unprivileged condition, when for instance they were almost certainly denied the chance of becoming literate. Accordingly, there were certainly considerations on her side of the question which made her attitude understandable, which made my retort to it somewhat uncomfortable and apologetic.

All the same, I believe that the retort which I made is the only right and possible one: Chaucer and Shakespeare and Milton, Edmund Spenser and Ben Jonson and John Donne, John Dryden and Alexander Pope are as much yours as they are mine—*if you want them*. Whatever we may think of the literature produced in the United States in the hundred years after the Declaration of Independence, it is surely nonsensical to speak of an American literature, as distinct from and foreign to English literature, at any period before 1776. And yet I get the strong impression that this, as it seems to me, self-evident truth is not one that is generally recognized. There come into my hands anthologies of American literature, designed for classroom use, which start with a section called "The Colonial Period," in which appear selections from Ann Bradstreet, Edward Taylor, Jonathan Edwards, Phyllis Wheatley, to go no further. Yet it must surely be the case that if before 1776 Milton and Shakespeare and Donne are yours as much as they are mine, so Anne Bradstreet and Edward Taylor and Jonathan Edwards are as much mine as they are yours. My students stare at me in surprise when I point out that in the one hundred and fifty years between the landing of the Pilgrim Fathers and the Declaration of Independence very few people of Caucasian race, born and living in the territory of what is now the continental United States, conceived of themselves as anything but Englishmen who happened to live on the opposite side of the Atlantic from most of their compatriots. Yet so far as I can see (I stand ready to be corrected) this was indeed the case. Indeed, those very Americans who themselves created the American nation as a political identity distinct from the British, the very fathers of the Republic themselves—Ben Franklin, John Adams, Thomas Jefferson—conceived of themselves, at least up to 1776, as Englishmen who happened to live overseas. How could they have thought otherwise?

So far as I can see, however, the colonial period is passed over rather rapidly in most surveys of American literature. I seem to detect a general consensus that American literature proper begins in the postrevolutionary period, with Philip Freneau or Washington Irving or Fenimore Cooper, and that it gathers speed and impetus only with Emerson, Emily Dickinson, Herman Melville, Walt Whitman. But this surely has the alarming effect of drastically foreshortening the cultural and historical experience of mankind in North America. Leaving aside the admittedly special case of the native Americans (the Amerindians), we can say that mankind in North America did in fact experience in some sort those two phases of European culture to which we give the names of the Age of the Baroque and the Age of the Enlightenment. But there is, I sometimes think, a general conspiracy to ignore these experiences, and to act as if the cultural memory of North American man reached back no further than to the romantic movement of the end of the eighteenth and the beginning of the nineteenth centuries. And this is, in at least one sense, flagrantly and demonstrably untrue. No man has, it may be thought, a firmer claim to be a true American than John Adams, who helped draft the Declaration of Independence and lived to become second president of the United States; and if one consults the diaries which the young John Adams kept, while he was still a country lawyer in New England, long before he attained international reputation as a diplomat and revolutionary, one finds him recording in his diary his impressions (very intelligent and perceptive ones) of the poetry of Donne, of Pope, of Shakespeare—all of whom he takes to be, naturally enough, the poets of his nation. Indeed, the Declaration of Independence itself, and still more the Constitution of the United States, are self-evidently documents of that historical phase of Western culture which is defined as "the Enlightenment." Among the incidental advantages which just might be derived from the interminable Watergate investigations, there might emerge a necessity for every American to understand that, insofar as he is safeguarded by and depends upon the Constitution, he is an heir to the eighteenth century neoclassic Enlightenment at least as much as to the romantic movement.

But then, I ask with some diffidence, is there any anthology of American literature for classroom use which reproduces, among the monuments of literature produced in the United States, the Declaration of Independence or any part of the Constitution of the United States, or John Adams's *Discourses on Davila,* or even Thomas Jefferson's *Notes on Virginia*? There may be such anthologies, but I have not come across them. And this strikes me as odd. After all, nobody denies that in the canon of English literature there figure, as of right, the political pamphlets of Jonathan Swift, the political polemics and parliamentary orations of Edmund Burke. But so far as I can see, "American literature" is very seldom taken to include, as a distinct and ancient literary genre, political speculation and commentary and political oratory. Do any of the political writings or orations of Henry Clay, for instance, deserve inclusion in any respectably comprehensive and representative anthology of American literature? So far as I know, not only has the question never been answered, it has perhaps never been asked.

I have reached the point where, in my impertinent temerity, I am suggesting that, despite the man-hours now devoted over several decades to "American literature," rather few scholars have brought themselves to question highly questionable assumptions, both as to period and (still more momentously) as to genre or literary kind. Is it not the case that, through the now several decades since American literature was recognized as a respectable academic discipline, both in the United States and abroad, never a year has passed without new books and articles on

Herman Melville, Nathaniel Hawthorne, Stephen Crane, Ernest Hemingway, Emily Dickinson, Thoreau, Walt Whitman; but that, on the other hand, years and years go by without anyone's ever offering a new candidate for inclusion in the canon of what American literature is taken to consist of? It was Ezra Pound, that expatriate and maverick American, who insisted through year upon year that the letters exchanged between Thomas Jefferson and John Adams as old men were a monument of American literature as well as of American history; and what college text in American literature shows that its author has even considered Pound's contention, let alone acted upon it? The letters of Horace Walpole, Thomas Gray, William Cowper, John Keats (to go no further) are accepted classics of English literature, as the letters by Mme. de Sevigné are of French. Where are their American counterparts? Do they not exist? Or do they indeed exist, but have never been looked at, or never from this point of view? Even if we restrict ourselves to the arbitrarily accredited genres of poem, story, and drama, how long is it since any scholar of American literature put forward a candidate, a practitioner of any one of these genres, as meriting inclusion in the canon? So far as my admittedly imperfect information goes, I find I have to track back thirty or forty years, to find the late Yvor Winters proposing for inclusion in the canon of American poets Jones Very and Frederick Goddard Tuckerman—a contention which seems to have been neither straightforwardly denied nor gratefully acceded to, but rather considered, at least in some quarters, as a gratuitously annoying qualification of what was already a profitably going concern. (For, if Frederick Goddard Tuckerman was, as Yvor Winters contended, a remarkably serious and accomplished poet, this was for some scholars a confounded nuisance, since Tuckerman could be shown to have been in constant contact with, and emulation of, the British poet Alfred Lord Tennyson, whereas the accepted orthodoxy required it to be believed that in the mid-nineteenth century no American poet *could* attain to first-rate stature except by denying the validity of British models and British precedent, as Walt Whitman did.)

You will see in any case that I am trying to register my confused impression that we have, in what is commonly accepted as American literature, a literature in which the canon of classic works has never yet been established. I have no time to do more than glance at one more category of works as to which this question of classic status seems never to have been raised: bearing in mind how travel narratives so different as Kinglake's *Eothen* and Cobbett's *Rural Rides* have been accepted as classic in the canon of English literature, how can we fail to be surprised that scholars of American literature seem never to have looked from this point of view at books like Alexander Ross's *Adventures of the First Settlers on the Oregon or Columbia River* (1849), or William L. Manly's *Death Valley in '49. The Autobiography of a Pioneer* (1894)? The journals of Lewis and Clark, Ross's narrative, and Manly's, must serve as representative of a vast number of books along the same lines, of which some (it may be surmised) still exist only in manuscript. Who has looked at them all? And if some scholars have reviewed them all—including those published by the Hudson's Bay Company (for in relation to these works the distinction between Canadian and United States literature seems to be more than ever impracticable and fatuous)—who has looked at them with a view to their status *as literature*? This does not mean asking: Do they contain purple patches of self-consciously "fine" writing? The question is rather, I'd suggest: Were the writer's feelings and imagination engaged, no less than his solid good sense and scrupulous concern for accuracy? I will dare to go even a little further, and ask: Who, except for a few honorable eccentrics like Yvor Winters, and David Levin in his *History as Romantic Art* (1959), has considered *historiography* as a genre of literature magnificently practiced and adorned in North America by Washington Irving in his *History of Astoria,* by Bancroft and Prescott, by Motley and Parkman, and (I would add) Walter Prescott Webb? I can only report that in the first *Anthology of American Literature* which I take down from my shelves (by Thomas M. Davis and Willoughby Johnson, 1966), the only one of these authors who appears is Irving, and he is represented by—you guessed it—"Rip Van Winkle." If Gibbon and Macaulay are glories of English literature, are not Prescott and Parkman among the glories of American? For all practical purposes, apparently not, despite the lip service that is hastily paid them when their names are guiltily remembered.

I should like to offer very tentatively my guess as to why and how it is that "American literature" has flourished as an academic discipline for so long, without the canon of classic works in that literature ever being established or indeed enquired about. To do so I must revert to one of my earlier observations, when I proposed that caucasian man in North America had experienced both the Age of the Baroque and the Age of the Enlightenment, yet stubbornly denied having experienced any phase of Western culture earlier than the Romantic. I think it is true to say that the Romantic movement, as in the early nineteenth century the tide of it engulfed one Western literature after another, had the effect of blurring and ultimately destroying one after another of the distinctions on which rested the doctrine of genres, of literary kinds, as that doctrine had been elaborated and ambitiously systematized by the neoclassic theorists of the Renaissance.

The distinctions between idyll and eclogue, between elegy and complaint, between satire and lampoon—these distinctions, and the many more that might be cited, soon gave way in the early nineteenth century, under the interrelated and typically Romantic convictions (1) that artistic form was self-generating and "organic," and (2) that artistic style was above all distinctive and personal. Moreover, the Romantic and post-Romantic generations were, and have been up to our own day, particularly suspicious of those genres of literature which most manifestly called upon predetermined design and calculation as to overall structure, and on discursive reason as to method. It seems to me we may not need to look any further for the reason why the nineteenth century, not just in America but in Europe also (and certainly in England), could regard historiography and political oratory as being literature only "after a fashion," only, as it were, by special license. It is because the American insists on regarding *his* literature as wholly Romantic and post-Romantic, that he is unable even to contemplate the possibility that that literature includes the letters of Adams and Jefferson, the histories of Francis Parkman, or the political oratory of Daniel Webster or Henry Clay.

What is so baffling about this for the Englishman is that, if I may reiterate, eighteenth-century habits of thought and language persist in American public life as they do not in the public life of England. The Constitution of the United States was framed according to eighteenth-century pre-Romantic ideals, and is couched in eighteenth-century Enlightenment language. By contrast, the English system of government, the English ideas of how society is ordered, though they were given an eighteenth-century face-lift by John Locke, in fact derive by slow incremental process from medieval times, and found their most impassioned apologist in Edmund Burke, who extolled them on grounds that most people would agree to describe as Romantic-reactionary. Thus it ought to be the case that it is the Englishman who finds it hard to sympathize with the Enlightenment frame of mind, whereas the American has ready access to it. But this is far from being the case. It would be wrong to say the very opposite is true, for in fact most Englishmen *do* find it hard to sympathize, except very shallowly, with the eighteenth century and what it stands for in the history of Western man. Yet that the American should refuse to sympathize with his own pre-Romantic past, to the extent of denying (unless he is a constitutional lawyer or a professional historian) that he has any eighteenth-century past at all—this cannot fail to astonish us. Pope and Dryden, Fielding and Goldsmith, ought to be *more* your authors than they are mine, simply because the institutionalized public life of your nation has kept open avenues of access to their imaginative and intellectual world, in a way that the public life of England has not.

What reasons there can be for such an extravagant cover-up, for denying that colonial North America ever had an Enlightenment culture, whereas in fact the polity of the United States is a product of that culture—this is a question which I cannot answer, and must leave aside. But that the cover-up exists I think cannot be doubted. The most astonishing proof of it came into my hands a short time ago, in the shape of a book lately published in New York, *America: A Prophecy*, edited by George Quasha and Jerome Rothenberg. This is an anthology which advertises itself with justice as "A New Reading of American Poetry from Pre-Columbian Times to the Present." It makes for fascinating reading, and is obviously the product of much curious learning. Perhaps the most immediately striking feature of it is what might be expected from the collaboration of Mr. Rothenberg: the inclusion of many pieces (few of them strictly "poems" in the perhaps too narrow sense we usually give to that word), which are translated from Iroquois, Sioux, Navajo, and other Native American languages, including languages from south of the border, such as Maya, Toltec, and Aztec (nothing, on the other hand, from the Spanish of Central America—which may seem odd). However, for my present purposes the most striking fact is that, of the more than three hundred items in this anthology, just *six* were written in English in North America before 1800. Six, out of more than three hundred! And of these six the four most substantial and interesting pieces—by John Fiske, Cotton Mather, and Edward Taylor—in fact represent what I have called, perhaps unhelpfully, the *baroque* rather than the Enlightenment; that is to say, they are clearly products of seventeenth-century habits of thought, not of those eighteenth-century ways of thinking which impelled Adams and Jefferson and Washington, James Madison and John Jay and Alexander Hamilton. This slanting of the evidence is too marked to be accidental. It must have been intended, and indeed so it was. For Quasha and Rothenberg take not just their title but, as they explain very lucidly, all the assumptions on which they structure their book from the writings of William Blake, that English poet who pronounced a relentless anathema on the thought and art of the century to which he was born, with its Enlightenment culture. William Blake, I should say, nowadays provokes more enthusiasm in North America than any other British poet whatever. And we begin to see why: Blake it is who tells the American that he not only may but must ignore the Enlightenment culture which informed and shaped the American Republic. It is an odd state of affairs, to say the least of it.

However that may be, I should like now to suggest that

the theory of American literature which I have been hesitantly sketching explains also another very striking feature of that literature as it is customarily presented to us: its being much of the time a parade of giants, a star show with hardly any supporting cast. Please notice that I speak only of American literature *as it tends to be presented to us.* It is not the case that American literature lacks figures in, as it were, the middle distance, writers who are estimable and memorable, even irreplaceable, though of something less than giant stature. A host of names comes to mind, across the generations: William Cullen Bryant and Frederick Goddard Tuckerman, Edith Wharton and Willa Cather, Hamlin Garland and Sarah Orne Jewett, Glenway Wescott and Wallace Stegner . . . and how many more? (I name only those to whom I'm immediately aware of feeling grateful.) All these writers, I believe, have secured a place in what may one day be acknowledged as the canon of American literature. But I think it is not writers like these, writers of this stature, whom we think of first when we say "American literature." The writers we think of first are the titanic figures that march, one after another, across the foreground. Emerson and Thoreau, Hawthorne and Melville, Whitman, even in her own way Emily Dickinson, even in his own way Poe—these are indeed gigantesque figures, larger than life. I think we have difficulty, though, in remembering that each of them had contemporaries, writers who deserve to be honored though they are very different from these Prometheans, certainly not giants and yet not dwarves either. And I use the word "Promethean" advisedly, and the word "titanic" also; for the difficulty we have in placing and justly esteeming the minor American classics, the minor masters who set themselves and secured limited but valuable objectives, can be rather easily related to the characteristically Romantic view of the agonized and untamable artist as Prometheus—with its implication that one "goes for broke" or not at all; that a modest or limited achievement is almost worse than no achievement whatever; that the only honorable ambition is to be a *great* writer, not just a good one. What bears this out, I suggest, is that we experience a similar difficulty in the Romantic and post-Romantic phases of other literatures besides American; in English literature, for instance, Walter Savage Landor and Robert Bridges and Mrs. Gaskell are writers of less than giant stature whom we are continually forgetting about, whom we cannot find a place for when we are reminded of them. In both literatures we are really much happier with, and more confident about, writers of another sort again—those who rather plainly aimed at gigantesque or titanic structure, as we see from the copiousness and variety of their "output," but who failed, more or less narrowly, to "make the grade." A James Fenimore Cooper, a Henry Wadsworth Longfellow, a Theodore Dreiser—those who scored a near miss, the failed or imperfect titans, giants brought low (more or less honorably) by Jacks who climbed the beanstalk after them . . . we find it easier to admire the flawed achievements of such writers than the relatively flawless but more limited achievement of a minor master such as (to name one from our own day) Janet Lewis. And this is because, whether we know it or not, we approach literature with Romantic assumptions and Romantic expectations.

As I draw to the end of these remarks, I cannot dispel from my mind something that perhaps has been growing in your minds as you have listened: the possibility that I have been on the wrong track from the first and all along; that by making play with such ideas as "the canon" and "the classic" I have only convicted myself of approaching a non-European literature with European assumptions and concepts that just don't apply as soon as the critic or literary historian crosses the Atlantic to the New World. After all, I cannot but reflect that the only notable occasion on which the word "classic" was applied to American literature was when it was used by a *British* writer, D. H. Lawrence, in his *Studies in Classic American Literature*. I have, however, come across the term being used by an American writer. This writer was William Carlos Williams, who wrote: "The future American poetry has to arise from speech—American, not English . . . from what we *hear* in America. Not, that is, from a study of the classics, not even the American 'classics'—the dead classics . . . which we have *never heard* as living speech. No one has ever heard them as they were written any more than we can hear Greek." In this American voice, as I hear it speak to me off the page, the word "classic" plainly is uttered with a contemptuous ring to it, such as it does not have in the English voice of D. H. Lawrence, taunting and sardonic as that voice often was. To opt for the spoken language so uncompromisingly as Williams does here, and in similar passages, is to deny that past generations of writing have any relevance at all to American writing today. (Williams's own writing now belongs to the American past; so presumably on his own showing his writings might as well be, and perhaps ought to be, forgotten.) This is to deny any continuity between one generation and the next; it is to make the history of American poetry a disconnected series of ever new starts, and I will readily confess that I am too European in grain to be able to come to terms with such a possibility. Of such a literature one could not write a history, only a chronicle. If that were the sort of literature that American literature is, I should be much less interested in it than in fact I am. I have to believe, and I think I begin to discern, that there is a continuity in

American literature, as in any European literature that I know of; that there can be discerned, running throughout, a tradition, or else several traditions alternating and sometimes conflicting. If so, then a history of that literature—as distinct from a mere chronicle—becomes a possibility. What I have been suggesting in the last few minutes is that the present climate of opinion about American literature seems to be such that the literary history I've been envisaging won't be written at all soon, if only because at present the *dis*continuities seem to be emphasized more than the continuities. ("Recurrence" is another matter: recurrent *patterns* in American literature can be, and often are, discerned—but such recurrences and repetitions in fact testify to discontinuity, not to a continuous and evolving *tradition*.)

I will end by expressing two hunches: (1) that the sort of continuity I have in mind may be in fact carried by minor writers rather than major ones; and (2) that it may be carried, not just by prose writers rather than poets, but by discursive and analytical and expository prose rather than by narrative prose, especially when that narrative prose is as "poetic" as the prose of Herman Melville on the one hand, Ernest Hemingway on the other. You will notice how each of these propositions has to do with the points that I made earlier in these remarks. And neither of them, surely, is at all novel or startling. The first rests upon the obvious fact that genius is often idiosyncratic. A major writer, therefore, by the very fact of his genius, is likely to be "off center." A Milton or a Melville does not merely rise above the tradition which he adorns; he pushes it askew under the force of the highly personal vision which he compels it to incorporate. The tradition therefore may be carried more securely by writers with less talent and less urgency. And my second proposition is likewise far from new. It was expressed with memorable force more than sixty years ago, by J. S. Phillimore:

> Poetry is a wind that bloweth where it listeth; a barbarous people may have great poetry, they cannot have great prose. Prose is an institution, part of the equipment of a civilization, part of its heritable wealth, like its laws, or its system of schooling, or its tradition of skilled craftsmanship.

Phillimore wrote thus in an essay, in the *Dublin Review* of 1913, on "Blessed Thomas More and the Arrest of Humanism in England." And the sentences were quoted by R. W. Chambers in *The Continuity of English Prose from Alfred to More and his School*, where I found them. This makes it plain that Phillimore, and Chambers after him, had in mind not the prose of novelists, not narrative prose at all unless it were the prose of travelers and historians, but rather discursive and expository prose. And this is my warrant for suggesting that if the time ever comes when students of American literature are more interested in its continuities than its discontinuities, they will do well to look for them in literary genres other than those of poem, story, or drama—precisely, in fact, in those genres which American literature, as commonly taught, appears not to possess. I do not need to underline the fact that, if Phillimore is right, such an investigation would be a study not just of North American literature but of North American *civilization*.

Some Notes on Rhythm in Verse

1. The frontier between free verse and metered verse is a great deal cloudier and more smudged than people seem to think. If you shorten an iambic measure to the trimeter, and then allow yourself all the liberties that traditional prosody allows you, you have a measure which few readers will scan, even subconsciously. For them the verse might as well be, and to all intents and purposes *is*, "free"; for you, the writer, the scanning of it is (if you want it that way) a sort of crutch or scaffolding in the act of composition, and thereafter (for whatever satisfaction you may get from this) a technical secret which you share only with your professional peers.

2. *A fortiori*, the distinction between accentual-syllabic verse and accentual verse (I use Yvor Winters's terminology, much the simplest and best that I know), a distinction that is crucial in longer measures like the pentameter, can become unimportant and indeed inapplicable when the measure is shortened. This interests me because I am aware of having gradually shortened, over twenty years of writing, my "standard" measure from pentameter

---

These notes first appeared in *Agenda,* Autumn/Winter 1972-73.

through tetrameter to trimeter. And I see that this has been a cautious but consistent movement towards "freedom."

3. Moreover, it seems to follow that you may write a passage of verse which can in fact be scanned, although for you, in the act of writing it, it is "free." If you are not scanning it as you write, then so far as you are concerned it is nonmetrical. This is a dangerous observation, for some of the sloppiest verse one encounters has been perpetrated by people who thought they were writing free verse when in fact they were writing, for instance, loose pentameters. And in general there is no excuse for not knowing what you are doing. All the same, the freedom of free verse is not always something that can be objectively determined by the reader but is, at least in some cases, the perhaps illusory sense of freedom that the writer has as he writes.

4. True free verse, as I have experienced it in the act of writing it, seems bound up with *improvisation*, with "keeping it going now that it has started." Writing it, you must not be interrupted, and for long stretches you cannot afford to take a break. For this reason I think of free-verse composition as musical, whereas metrical composition lends itself to a steadily punctuated building up, block by block, architectural; metered verse can go into stanzas—free verse never can.

5. *Rhythm*, in free verse and metered verse alike, is determined as much by syntax as by lineation. An advertisement on a hoarding or in a newspaper, if it is written in sentences and strung across lines of unequal length, has as much rhythm, and just the same sort of rhythm, as a passage of free verse. That is not to say, of course,

that the rhythm it has will be satisfying or significant, though in fact in an advertisement that is meant to be "catchy" the rhythm will satisfy, if at a merely rudimentary level. Alike in the advertisement and the poem, the rhythm is determined very largely by the spacing and placing of pauses—the pauses of different weight and duration signaled by comma, semicolon, colon, full stop, by line ending without punctuation stop, line ending with comma, line ending with colon, and so on. This is so elementary that it should not need saying; but it does have to be said, as I know. Finer gradations of pause (too fine for me to attempt to measure them) can be signalized and achieved in writing which has taken note of Pound's precedent, by indentations (of many spaces or of few), by the oblique stroke on the typewriter, and by other devices of spacing provided by typewriter and typesetter; but these are refinements or grace notes. The basic stave or paradigm is still determined by (1) the verse line, (2) the sentence.

6. As I have argued elsewhere, such an understanding of rhythm reveals as wholly misconceived the objection to free verse that it is "merely-chopped-up prose." (Answer: of course it is—has the chopping up been done with wit and feeling, to create a satisfying rhythm?) A variant objection is that rhythms have been created by devices which are "merely typographical." (Retort: why "merely"?)

7. Metered verse in stanzas can use the stanza itself as a rhythmical unit, superadded to the free-verse units of the sentence and the verse line. And this is what I most like to do myself: if I can arrange my trimeters in five-line or six-line stanzas (rhymed or unrhymed), I can draw on all the rhythmical resources of free verse or the

blank-verse paragraph, and yet be free of another range of rhythmical shapes altogether. It is a way of being musician and architect at once. But of course only some experiences will allow of this sort of treatment; to render experiences of other sorts I am glad to have at hand both free verse and the so often damned but still enduring blank-verse pentameter.

Talking with Dana Gioia

Let me begin by asking you a question about the direction of modern English poetry. Did you read the essay Robert Lowell wrote for the American Poetry Review *about Philip Larkin's* Oxford Book of Twentieth Century English Verse?

Yes, I did.

I'd like to ask you a question about something Lowell said in that essay, which, I believe reflects the attitude many American readers have about contemporary British poetry. Americans, even cosmopolitan ones like Lowell, often criticize British poets, especially ones like Larkin, or the current poet laureate, John Betjeman, or even you, as having retreated from the world at large. Whereas earlier British poets spoke for England as one of the centers of the world, now they have shrunken to the stature of local poets who take for granted a diminished and defeated England robbed of its Empire and uncertain of its place in the world. How would you answer this criticism?

This interview took place in Stanford, California, in 1977, and first appeared in *Sequoia* 22, no. 2 (Winter 1978). © 1977 Associated Students of Stanford University.

I would answer that it's very ungracious indeed because I believe it is true of Larkin and Betjeman and not of me.

[Laughs.] *Next question: Is there currently a tradition, do you feel, being carried out in British verse?*

No . . . not any more than I think there is in America. Perhaps everybody feels like this at times. The poetic landscape . . . I find it impossible to find any features in it. It's not that there isn't the talent, but in both places the talents seem to be running every which way. It seems to me a sort of eclecticism—anything goes, both in technique and in subject matter. There are those, there have been for several years really in England (they're still around) who say—oh yes, we do have a tradition and we define it as precisely that which the American modern isn't. We are talking about a native tradition (they say) which has survived all through the supposed modernist revolution of Eliot and Pound, which may have been lost to sight for a while during the preeminence of Eliot, but which in fact was always there. And this tradition is to be traced in names like Hardy above all, and perhaps Walter de la Mare, and a poet of the First World War who certainly is too little heard of in the United States, a really beautiful poet named Edward Thomas; and then to Robert Graves and then it's propped up by names like Philip Larkin and, you know, give or take a few other names. . . . This is plausible. It's a plausible argument. I don't personally believe in it, and I think it's bad for the English to believe in it, because it encourages them to think that in some way they have been comfortably insulated from what we think of as the modernist revolution not just in poetry but in all the arts, indeed in the sensibility and the technology and the rest. It *cannot* be true that England is left out. Since all the other psychological and historical and political changes have hit England and changed the sensibility of the English, how *can* they have escaped the modernist revolution in the arts?

Do you personally feel that you are working outside any tradition that you feel at home with, or that you have to create your own tradition? Or is this a stupid question?

I don't think it's a stupid question. I was schooled to think that Mr. Eliot had said the last word about tradition, and I'm not sure that he didn't. I think a lot of things that I understand he said about tradition are right. I take him to have said that every major poet at any time creates his own tradition for himself. That is to say, he's the heir to all the poetry that's ever been written in the English language. But in that enormous resource of precedents, he gradually sorts out those which he can in fact make use of in his own writing (not necessarily those most esteemed)—that's what a tradition is. It seems to me that yes, I've done that, but then, as I say, any poet worth his salt has done the same.

What is your *tradition?*

Heigh-ho. Wow, I don't know. Hmm. We don't, we won't, worry about tradition across languages, we're not talking about Pasternak, people like that, we're talking about English-language poets. Well, it goes along the way of what I *conceive* to be my tradition, that I am aware of Ben Jonson, Andrew Marvell, John Dryden, Goldsmith, Cowper, Wordsworth . . . and—that'll do for the time being.

You've often been associated with the so-called Movement of Philip Larkin, Kingsley Amis, John Wain, Elizabeth Jennings; and currently you edit a partisan quarterly called Poetry Nation Review. *Do you look upon yourself as having been, or as being, a part of any particular movement or school or alliance?*

Yes, there was a time when I was, and indeed it's now got itself a modest little place in literary history, and is called simply The Movement, with a capital *M*; and it belongs to the middle 1950s, to a period when I discovered, and half a dozen other poets subsequently my friends discovered, that though we were starting from very different points we were moving upon a common area, a point at which our different careers, and the styles we were working out for ourselves, intersected in an important way. And that moment in history is marked by what was the fighting anthology of the Movement, *New Lines*, edited by Robert Conquest who's now out here at the Hoover Institution. And then, in the nature of things, the alliance rapidly disintegrated, the individual talents diverged. It wasn't like a Parisian French movement, you know, it wasn't actually dreamed up with a manifesto all afloat around a café, and so it didn't break up in vituperations on matters of abstract principle. Simply, it happened, then it dissolved itself. It's still true that some of those poets, most of those poets within *New Lines*, I still have considerable affection for; and I am always interested in their writing, where they're going, or seem to be going. I have a natural sympathy with them, though some of them now seem to be writing very differently from me. In fact one wishes that that sort of thing happened more often. Others have said this. People who weren't in The Movement, younger people who were hardly even born then, have said that they wished something like that would happen to us now, because at any rate it would make sense of the poetic landscape. That landscape would not be totally eclectic, there would be something there, whether you agreed or disagreed with it; there would be something to focus on. If there did emerge such a movement in which variously talented but serious writers clung to their little things in common for a while, this would be a very good thing. I suppose it would be a very good thing in American poetry too. Because America is so much larger, so much more populous, possesses so many more poets, and it seems harder for the poets to get in touch with each other, the likelihood of that sort of thing in American poetry is less great, I suppose; though you had the Black Mountain school that founded itself in the shadow of Charles Olson in the early 1950s. That seems to me a real "movement" of this sort, which was, for as long as it lasted, immensely influential on each of the talented and serious writers who were concerned with it.

Do you see the group of young poets and the older poets associated with Poetry Nation Review *as any sort of movement or school of poets with a common direction?*

No, I don't, but we must be clear about my association with that magazine. You're in a sense quite right to say that I edit it, since I am one of the three editors named on the masthead, but the effective editor, the managing editor, is Michael Schmidt who was out here and gave a reading about two years ago. He's a much younger man than me, he's just thirty. He is, oddly enough, American by conditioning, but Mexican by citizenship and an English resident by preference; which sounds very complicated and complex but yes, he was at Harvard before he went to Oxford and then after he'd been through Oxford he never went home again. I'm very devoted to him. My point is that, if there is such a movement forming up around that magazine, it's going to be Michael

Schmidt or somebody not of my generation who's going to discover it. It's the same with the other name on the masthead, C. H. Sisson, a very fine and a very *English* poet. Sisson and I, we are there as a sort of avuncular presence, to stop the frame of reference from being too time-bound to the 1970s.

[Laughs.] *Do you feel that in any way your early critical writings or your current critical writings, for example books like* Articulate Energy *or* Purity of Diction in English Poetry, *were manifestoes or defenses of your earlier writing?*

Yes, I sensed that when my first book, *Purity of Diction in English Poetry*, was reissued. It is, I can see now, and I think even when I wrote it I knew that it was, a sort of concealed manifesto. If it's academically respectable it served the purpose of advancing my academic career, but that wasn't its main purpose. And some of the other people involved in The Movement, like Kingsley Amis, recognized that.

I don't think the same about *Articulate Energy*. *Articulate Energy* is sort of an extension of *Purity in Diction* in the sense that I discovered even more troubling questions about the language and the culture I was writing in. I think *Articulate Energy* isn't a manifesto. Of the later books, the only one that has a trace of the manifesto is *Thomas Hardy and British Poetry*, which I wrote out here a few years ago. And that's a funny sort of manifesto because—though really I'm not ashamed of the book—it never makes up its mind whether it's addressing the American reader or the British reader, and part of the time it is castigating the Americans for not being British, and the rest of the time it's castigating the British for not being Americans. But there is a certain sort of manifesto quality about it. And it's principally concerned with coming to terms with the fact that one of the great poets of our century is Thomas Hardy. He is a great poet whom we invariably forget about, when we generalize about twentieth-century poetry.

Do you see any other overall relationship between your critical writing and your poetry?

Yes. Certainly the early critical books are related to the earlier poetry. I would say that I wrote the criticism in order to explain to myself what I had been doing in the poems. I did not write the criticism to decide what I ought to do and what I wanted the poems to do. That isn't the way it works. To that extent there is sense to all the sentimentality about poems, and what mysterious things they are, how they happen and you don't know why. There is that element of hardheaded truth about "inspiration."

So in some sense your criticism is an attempt to answer problems that suggested themselves in the process of writing?

Yes.

At Stanford you're one of the people in charge of the graduate verse writing program and you have taught poetry writing courses as long as you've been here. How do you see your role as a teacher of poetry writing?

Well, certainly a teacher of creative writing is a teacher in quite a different sense from a teacher of biochemistry, a teacher of history, or even a teacher of eighteenth-century literature. It is a much more elusive and complicated relationship that you have with your students when you're teaching writing, and in many ways it is more rewarding and in many ways too it is far more emotionally draining. On the one hand in the formal workshop sessions I regard myself as merely holding the ring around something like a dozen people criticizing each other. As I run it, that criticism has to be very strictly controlled, that is to say I hold the reins very tight. You know this, Dana, because you've taken a course from me. I don't let the author of the poems being discussed join in the discussion of them. He or she has to sit silent while other people discuss, and I think this is crucial. It is very difficult for people to do this to each other. What you've done, if the device succeeds, is to create artificially a situation which will never recur any other time in any writer's life—a chance of hearing certain reasonably intelligent and certainly concerned readers arguing about a piece of his writing, and him eavesdropping upon them. This will never happen again; and this is a purely artificial situation in which a poet meets his or her audience. I am merely there to set up that situation and to keep it within reasonably strict control. And the other part of it of course is in consultancy sessions when people show me poems. I keep them for a week or two weeks, and then we come in and talk about them, and I give them my ideas about their poems. Here it seems to me that the relationship is that of a master to an apprentice. I like to think of it being like Ghirlandaio in his workshop. And as we all know, in that workshop (for which for some reason we always use the French word *atelier*), were young apprentices learning at the master's feet. In fact there are paintings that are just called "school of Ghirlandaio." And the school includes painters who are going to be infinitely more talented than the master is. But all you have to teach in this situation is the result of having been at this particular game for twenty years longer than the pupil has. All you can hope to transfer is the results of your own experience. And the only rules there are in a situation like that are such "rules" as when you say, "Well, when something like this happens to me in a poem, this is what I tend to do about it"; or "If this poem were mine I would be inclined to see if I could do this, this, or this to it." These are merely rules of thumb. People misunderstand these things. If there were a relation where there was surefire technique, a body of surefire techniques, comprehending everything from meter to diction to subject matter and so on, which I had in my possession and could transmit, then we would not be dealing with an art at all; there would merely be a sort of craft, a rather lowly sort of craft. We hope that here at Stanford we are aware of the danger of giving that impression.

At Stanford I believe you have the same chair that the late Yvor Winters had . . . .

No, that is not true.

But basically you have the same position in the Department that he had, in some ways. . . .

I think that's true, yes.

Do you feel in any way that you're carrying on or quarreling with his continuing presence at Stanford? Or of a school of poets at Stanford that he began?

No. Yvor Winters I'm proud to say was a much valued older friend of mine. I was never his pupil, and indeed our relationship began with my writing a fan letter to him when I was a graduate student at Cambridge University. I did meet him off and on over the years after that. And certainly, when the chance came to come to Stanford, the fact that I would in some sort be taking on Winters' mantle and perpetuating the work that he'd started here was part of the attractiveness. I would like to believe, if he were regarding us from the shades, and saw the sort of things that have gone on in the nine years when Kenneth Fields and I for the most part have been doing the work that Winters used to do, that he would not disapprove. I'd like to believe so. Mr. Winters himself, like anybody else, of course changed over his lifetime. Towards the end of life he was a tired man and a sick man, and in many ways a justifiably disappointed man. He was more impatient of varieties of writing and varieties of temperament than he was when he was younger. At that time his canons of approved writing in the present as in the past were too narrow and too strict for me to agree with. But this was his last phase. I think he was at his best both as a poet and a critic when he was younger. I don't mean when he was a young man, but when he was in his maturity, not when he was old and failing. Some of the people who studied with him early and late, I do know. They're valued acquaintances of mine. Some of them, I know, do feel that insofar as I've exerted any influence at all it has been towards an altogether excessive liberalizing of what was Winters' last position. Others, I think, don't think that. They believe it is a loyal and natural development out of Winters' legacy. I'd like to believe the same.

Finally, can you make any comparisons or contrasts between the way that you as a young man learned to write poetry, and developed as a writer, and the way that your American students do?

Yes, I can! It seems to me (I could be wrong about this), but it seems to me that as a young poet, I lost more time than I needed to. I wasted more years than I need have wasted, for lack of any institution to which I could turn; the lack of any *atelier*, if I could again use that word. The prevailing conviction in England, which still survives there, is that there is no teaching of these matters; that it is wholly amateur and nonprofessional, that everyone must find out for himself. Now, if that is the English vice, there is of course the corresponding American vice. The American vice is an excessive professionalism, which thinks that it's all a matter of technical know-how which you just have to master, and then away you go. I'm certain that there are some "creative writing" schools around the country which do their pupils more harm than good. Nonetheless, they *should* exist on most university campuses. If there had been anything comparable in my English university when I was a younger man, with a bit of luck I do believe I could have saved myself some time. I could have saved myself going up blind alleys. This seems to me the most that a creative writing teacher can do for the people that are in his class. He can say: "I wouldn't pursue that game much further if I were you, because I've been up there and it ends in a bare wall."

ISBN 0-472-06310-3

DONALD DAVIE

Trying to Explain

Trying to Explain gathers a new collection of Donald Davie's essays on poetry and poets. Writing as a British poet who spends most of his time in the United States, Davie analyzes major voices in the poetic tradition of England, Ireland, and America. His ranging intelligence urges the reader to consider poetry from a different and useful perspective.

Poets on Poetry collects critical books by contemporary poets, gathering together the articles, interviews, and book reviews by which they have articulated the poetics of a new generation.

Other books in the series:

DONALD HALL	*Goatfoot Milktongue Twinbird*
DAVID IGNATOW	*Open Between Us*
GALWAY KINNELL	*Walking Down the Stairs*
MAXINE KUMIN	*To Make a Prairie*
WILLIAM STAFFORD	*Writing the Australian Crawl*
DIANE WAKOSKI	*Toward a New Poetry*

Please write for information on available editions and current prices.

The University of Michigan Press   Ann Arbor